From Glass Slipper to Glass Ceiling

Your Personal Guide to Becoming Empowered and Shattering the Proverbial Glass Ceiling

Cristina Carballo-Perelman, M.D.

From Glass Slipper to Glass Ceiling

COPYRIGHT © 2019

PAPERBACK ISBN: 978–0-9984178-5-1

EBOOK ISBN: 978-0-9984178-6-8

Library of Congress Control Number 2015914893

Printed in the United States of America

Previously Published as CALLING ALL WOMEN

PUBLISHER: CCP ENTERPRISES, LLC

ALL RIGHTS RESERVED. NO PART OF THIS PUBLICATION MAY BE REPRODUCED OR TRANSMITTED IN ANY FORM OR BY ANY MEANS, ELECTRONIC OR MECHANICAL, INCLUDING PHOTOCOPY, RECORDING, OR ANY INFORMATION STORAGE RETRIEVAL SYSTEM, WITHOUT PERMISSION IN WRITING FROM THE COPYRIGHT OWNER.

Table of Contents

Dedication..v

Foreword vii

Introduction xv

Part I: History of the Glass Ceiling 1

Chapter One: *Equality of the Sexes: What Equality Really Means* 2

Chapter Two: *Progress for Women in the Field of Medicine and the Corporate World* 15

Chapter Three: *Progress for Women in Underdeveloped Countries* 33

Chapter Four: *How World Religions Demonize the Female Figure: Past and Present* 43

Chapter Five: *Why Men Still Rule the World—for Now* 53

Chapter Six: *How and Why Little Girls Grow Up Unempowered: A Pediatrician's Perspective* 57

Part II 65

Chapter Seven: *The Original Fairy Tale Nightmare* 66

Part III 71

Chapter Eight: *The Eleven Attributes of Empowered Women* 72

Chapter Nine: *Exude Confidence* 77

Chapter Ten: *Work as Part of the Team But Maintain Your Visionary Goal* 89

Chapter Eleven: *Respect Others But Never Compromise* 101

Chapter Twelve: *Be Compassionate and Show Empathy* 115

Chapter Thirteen: *Be Humble and Know You Are Constantly Learning* 127

Chapter Fourteen: *Stay Calm During Times of Stress* 135

Chapter Fifteen *Acknowledge Others* 141

Chapter Sixteen: *Be Honest* 149

Chapter Seventeen: *Demonstrate Courage* 159

Chapter Eighteen: *Achieve Success* 167

Chapter Nineteen: *Enjoy Your Work* 175

Part IV 181

Chapter Twenty: *The Modern Day Fairytale* 182

Chapter Twenty-One: *Final Thoughts* 189

About the Author 193

Dedication

I dedicate this book first to my husband, Alvin. Without him, I would never have clearly seen the differences between respect and placation; equal rights and expected role-playing; love and servitude.

He has shown me that men and women can be respectful of each other as well as share in family and work responsibilities, while working together toward the common goal of enjoying the journey.

He's given me hope that there are many men out there who respect women as equals and strive to make a better world for our children with positive role models.

It's because of his support that I can write this book with the confidence of knowing that I speak the truth—and the truth shall set us free.

Although the title of the book implies I want women around the world to take over, what I really strive for is that we will one day be seen as equals. I want us to take back our lives as equal members of society, and be able to fully participate in the success and growth of our civilization so our children can live in a more peaceful world.

To my love, my equal partner, and soul mate—thank you.

I would also like to dedicate this book to my daughter, Rachel, who has looked up to me as a working mom, and has inspired me to be the best that I can be in everything I do. This book is meant to help guide her and her girlfriends who might find themselves in similar quandaries during their professional lives. I hope that I can instill in them the confidence necessary to be partners and mothers, and to also have fulfilling careers without feeling the need to compromise or to set priorities as to which is more important. I've been very blessed to have it all. I can only hope that the world continues to improve its egalitarian stance and allow our young women to blossom to their full potential.

To my parents, who taught me from a very young age that I was able to become anything I wanted to be, and that being a female was not a deterrent. They allowed and encouraged me to pursue my dreams and not once brought up the subject of marriage or their expectations of it. They always made sure I understood that I needed to stand on my own two feet, independent of any other person for happiness or success.

Finally, I would like to dedicate this book to all the confident, courageous women from the past who paved the way to where we find ourselves at present and to the women seeking further guidance as they lead us into the future.

Foreword

My inspiration to write this book came from my life experiences—including my love of fairy tales. Perhaps, early on, I saw the attributes of empowered women in these stories and subconsciously I took to heart the lessons they taught. I'm also very proud of our legacy, created by the women who have come before us and who blazed the trail of empowerment and equality.

After all, if we look at the history of our human development, women have progressed from living in a cave, making meals from meat brought to us to cook, to being considered goddesses in some of the early ancient religions. However, at some point, we lost this goddess status and, during the time period prior to the suffrage movement, we ended up relegated to a subservient role. Somehow, we re-found our way toward the path of equality and into the era of bra-burning, better known as "Women's Lib." Unfortunately, we may be taking some steps backwards when we consider current culture in which a popular best seller gives us permission—even encourages us—to be the submissive partner waiting for the next risqué sexual encounter. Advertisements glorifying the perfect female physique have not championed our cause either.

So, what happened to us? What happened to the equality between sexes in all areas, from raising kids to being active participants in the boardroom? Why is it now okay for us to play the submissive role in the bedroom? If we continue to perpetuate that this message is acceptable because it's published and a best seller, then this will become the new normal and our new reality.

I'm here to protest against this new affront to our rights as human beings who have brains as well as breasts and butts.

It's because of this trend that I wanted to actually sit down and write this book. I wanted to help women finally become empowered in their lives.

As an example, Sheryl Sandberg, the COO of Facebook and author of *Lean In*, continues, in my opinion, to throw the collective "us" under the bus by suggesting that perhaps the reason we're not treated as "equal" with the men around the table—and therefore don't advance to positions of leadership—is because we're the ones holding ourselves back. We choose to play second fiddle; we sabotage our strengths and instead highlight our weaknesses. What weaknesses, you may ask? According to Ms. Sandberg, the list includes: being married, having children and dealing with the accompanying childcare issues, and being responsible for maintaining a home. All of these are holding us back.

Her message to women is mixed. While she believes we need to find partners who help us succeed in our careers, she also believes that we also must be aggressive and act like men, i.e., raise our hands in the boardroom and "keep our hands up" no matter what is taking place in our personal lives. We must take care of our personal issues only after we have actively engaged in our work world and committed our time there first. If I understand her correctly, our personal lives should have a lower priority than our work if we want to advance. She believes that because our personal lives take precedent over our careers, we may at first "put our hands up" in the boardroom, but quickly put them back down when we realize that our participation may impinge on our personal lives. The problem with this type of thinking is that, although it helps us as women to be more assertive and perhaps more visible and advance in our careers, what is the cost? What I believe is missing from her message is that careers deserve two equal partners to share in the personal responsibilities—thereby allowing the least amount of sacrifice to either partner's career or personal world.

She is correct that our personal lives get in the way of advancement. However, her solution would make the attainment of quality personal time almost obsolete. In her world, if a partner is unavailable to help out, we must rely on others. In her world, nannies could become the new six-figure-salary profession, based on the responsibilities they would need to assume—all so your career won't suffer. Do we really want other people taking care of our families? Do we really want a partner who takes over the childcare and housework at the expense of his career? I think either of these scenarios is less than ideal.

I believe I offer a different solution. While this solution does require male buy-in, it's as equals. We can't make it happen alone; not without significant compromise to the other person or your family.

All of this brings to the forefront the two following constructs. First, it's ridiculous that women's bodies are regarded as inferior equipment to cope in today's world. I would think that the ability to create life and feed that life without any store-bought products would automatically justify a certain level of respect, awe, and authority. Alas, that's not the case in today's world. In fact, for some, it seems to support the belief we are the weaker sex: too volatile, too emotional, too hysterical. PMS becomes the answer to why women cannot function in a "man's" world.

The second construct is the belief that it's only the woman's responsibility to raise the kids and maintain the house. Equal partnership goes beyond the workplace and should encompass all areas of life. Only then can we hope to be equal partners in all areas of life and enjoy them without compromise.

In the modern age, women should have an equal voice and equal rights in all aspects of life. I certainly feel that equality among the sexes should be the norm rather than the exception. The questions that beg answers still remain with us: Why should women be equals in the workplace and at home? What difference does it make in the scheme of individual lives, communities, or world well-being for women to be seen as equals?

I will strive to answer these in the coming pages.

Tragically, global rights for women—even an acknowledgement that women's rights are important—are lacking. Women still struggle, in both developed and underdeveloped countries, to be seen as valuable members of society. In fact, in some parts of the world, we struggle daily just so we can ensure that we—and our daughters—are respected as human beings and not treated like livestock.

My goal in writing this book is to put down on paper the attributes and habits that have helped me become more empowered. My hope is that by other women learning about and practicing these attributes—those in the workplace and at home who feel demeaned in their lives—their lives will improve. So, to all who hold this vision, I want to say, please read this book, become empowered, and gather the respect you deserve. And to those who feel they have achieved their goals and are considered empowered, it never hurts to review and refresh these ideas. Who knows? Perhaps new ideas will be garnered!

Let me tell you a little about myself and how I became so passionate about this topic.

My Personal Journey

My own history is that I am a female physician, a pediatrician specializing in sick infants, and have been for a little over a quarter century. Despite all the perceived equalities afforded women in different professions—including medicine—I still practice in a man's world. In fact, "The Good Ol' Boys Club" in both physician groups as well as medical administrators is still alive and very much the norm. It was frustration with this reality, coupled with the popular media's emphasis on women's bodies, demeaning fashions, and social expectations, that made me want to counter this.

My journey through this male-dominated world actually began in college when my advisor (a male) told me I would be better off following nursing (obviously, in his mind, a more traditional female role) than attempting to become a physician. He did nothing to help me on my journey to become an M.D. In fact, he tried to thwart it. This experience was further amplified in college during my freshman year when my male math teacher gave me an option to assure a better grade to help me on my quest to enter medical school—by providing certain services to him. As a young and naïve woman, I was so taken aback by both situations that I felt more determined than ever to prove them both wrong.

At the time, I didn't have the confidence to report these teachers and mentors to the college's administration. However, looking back, I don't believe much would have been done about it. After all, it was a different era, and I had no proof of what had been said to me. So I ignored them and continued to follow my dreams.

I refused to follow the traditional paths that women had been relegated to in the past. I didn't want to use anything but my brain to achieve my professional goals—and I certainly wasn't going to compromise my ethics to do so. As disappointing as these first lessons were in navigating a man's world, I took the bull by the horns and used grace and determination to empower myself and become a respected member of this society. I persevered and succeeded, but not without struggles. Along the way, I identified the attributes needed to empower myself. They were self-taught but true, and they proved to be the tools I needed to reach my goals.

After years and many experiences—my own and others—I was determined to put down my thoughts in order to share my experiences with other women who were also seeking empowerment. By incorporating fairy tales into my lessons, I hope to make these ideas easier to teach our children. After all, we've been exposed to these messages our whole lives, as have our children.

In addition to using examples from fairy tales, I have included well-known women as real-world examples of these empowering attributes in action.

As women, we need to be respected for our contributions at work and at home because doing so provides a role model for our daughters. It's my hope that future generations also will continue to benefit from these lessons. We can further capitalize on these lessons as the world benefits from the expertise of even more empowered women leaders.

I hope you enjoy my advice. I don't want women to be placed on pedestals or tied with satin to the bedposts. I also don't want women to have to choose between family and career. The fulfillment of both is nearly impossible without equality being part of the solution.

Instead, I'd like for us to be respected for our valuable input, perspectives, and ideas—and our ability to juggle family and work life with joy and grace, confident that we are true partners.

Introduction

Intel Corporation recently sponsored the 10x10 Girls Education Project. This Project suggests that girls shouldn't be—and aren't—what society thinks they are. Girls are actually the product of their own self-perceptions.

Initially, this seems to be a fantastic way to say that empowerment comes from within. The problem is that, despite how much a girl wants to see herself as empowered and an important member of society, she can't because she's been told otherwise her entire life.

Daniel Drubach talks about this concept in his article, "Judaism, Brain Plasticity and the Making of the Self." In it, he discusses how the brain is in a "constant state of structural and functional change," (*Journal of Religion and Health* 41, no.4 [Winter 2002] pp. 311–322) which allows experiences to shape the brain and create traits such as compassion, empathy, and honesty that may not be naturally present. Even if the brain doesn't have a particular personality trait, it can actually be trained to generate that trait if enough outside experiences affect its structure through neural connections.

In this book, I hope to help girls change their own internal perceptions—that may have been formed by outside sources—and create new perceptions of empowerment. Based on the theory of the mind's ability to create patterns of behavior, we can change girls' brain structures to believe they truly are empowered. Perhaps this, together with newly abundant media awareness and programs, will further empower young girls around the world, and will allow the true beauty in each girl and woman to more readily shine for the entire world to see.

In the first part of my book, I'll define what equality of the sexes really is, and how we, as empowered women, can help to make this goal a reality. These definitions and distinctions are an important foundation on which to build personal growth and to make the world a better place for everyone.

There is one point, I want to make crystal clear: I do not want women to aspire to become "little men." I want women to have equality with their male counterparts in socio-economics, educational opportunities, voting, and health. I want women to be empowered members of society, not powerful dictators over others.

I will also examine how the perception of women has changed over time, and how some countries fall far behind others in pursuit of equality between the sexes.

The next topic I'll tackle is why men outnumber women in positions of power.

While I strive to answer the question of equality throughout the book, I'm most interested in how we can change this perception and reality forever. I think we have a chance to create a new world for future generations. As a pediatrician, I also feel I have an obligation to give parents advice on how to raise children who have the skills and desire to create this new world. I have included a chapter on these recommendations.

If men and women are going to make this world a better place for our children, we must learn to work together with mutual respect for each other in all areas of life. Finally—and permanently—we must bury the notion that one gender is subservient to the other. We need to embrace our different strengths as equally important and complementary. Our different strengths are what create the best lifestyle for us and our children—and the world.

The second part of the book is structured a little differently. I explore how the original fairy tale is actually a nightmare. It's a story of a world very similar to the one we live in today. Unfortunately, this tale has no hero or heroines and has a sad ending. There is no "happily ever after" at the end. Instead it describes the reality we are facing in today's world when we consider the prevailing attitudes toward women. The similarities between this fairyland and our reality are startling, but important to understand.

I go on to use well-known fairy tales throughout the descriptions of the eleven attributes of empowered women because they are the first stories we hear as children and are perceived by our young minds as being magical. The time-honored stories in this collection of oral and written tales describe to us the differences between good and evil—right from wrong. Each has an imbedded moral compass that guides us as we navigate life's difficulties. These stories, each in their own way, set the stage as we talk about each attribute that, all together, make up empowered women.

At the start of each chapter, I describe the main character of a well-known story. We all know how fairy tales begin: "Once upon a time…" It's the beloved introduction that signals a "happily ever after" ending. In fact, critics of these fairy tales point out that these stories, simply read, have the effect of demeaning women, reducing them to simple-minded, helpless girls looking to be saved by their Prince Charming. The "happily ever after" actually implies salvation by the male hero of the story. Without these heroes, the female characters in these stories would wither away, lonely and useless to themselves and others.

I want to present a different side; a side that showcases evidence that our characters strongly demonstrate the attribute I'm ascribing to each of them. As someone once told me, the heroines in these stories didn't need to be saved. They were in situations that necessitated survival tactics and, therefore, *appeared* to be saved. In reality, they created their own salvation stories.

It's actually through these stories that we find the attributes important to survive and reach our goals.

This spin on these stories might seem strange, but I'd like us to challenge ourselves to look at them a little differently. If we can tell these stories—each emphasizing a hidden quality that the main female character has—we can better visualize the empowered woman materializing in front of us. She'll show us she isn't just another damsel in distress waiting for her Prince Charming.

At the end of each fairy tale, I take some literary liberty and create an alternate ending, highlighting what would happen if the attribute being talked about didn't exist in each of the particular characters. The contrast demonstrates the importance that each attribute contributes to the goal of becoming empowered.

By looking at the stories with new eyes, you could say that we've been reading these stories the wrong way and emphasizing the wrong qualities. By reading these stories with a new perspective, you might get a different read altogether.

If we can share these stories with our daughters, with the emphasis on the attributes listed—rather than the way they have been usually read, with the emphasis on the dysfunctional qualities—we'll create powerful examples to teach our daughters how to be empowered women.

In the end, as we examine the fairy-tale world, we finally understand that the women in these stories prove themselves through difficult trials and show us their true strengths.

Let me emphasize that these attributes aren't the sole property of women. The attributes that truly empower must exist in both men and women. In male leaders, these are more often than not expressed in a more masculine way, where power seems to be the vehicle through which they are played out. As we will examine further on, power is not the vehicle which I believe should drive these attributes to fruition. In women who want to be empowered at work and in their personal lives, some or all of these attributes are missing or poorly executed.

When we examine these attributes more closely, we actually start to see patterns that explain why some are more underdeveloped than others in women. I will describe the qualities these attributes must have so that both men and women can use them equally, with success. For now, I want to simply describe them and why they may be lacking in women and how they may appear in men.

The "Cliff-Notes" Version of the 11 Attributes That Empower Women and Men, Why They Are Important, and Why Some or All May Be Lacking in Women

1. Confidence: Without confidence, a person would not be able to voice their opinion because of fear of rejection or ridicule. As a woman, it would be hard to exude confidence if others, either men or women, shoot your confidence down every day. Less-confident women avoid confrontation and tend to back off into a corner. On the other hand, if a confident man's opinion were questioned, you would more likely see an immediate physical

response both in body language as well as voice volume. A man's confidence is rarely shaken.

2. Team Member: Being a valued team member is an important part of feeling empowered because your value is immediately evident. Working as part of a team, however, is challenging if your role has always been more of a server instead of a true team player. The examples of fetching coffee for others in the team or making copies for everyone are examples of servitude and not full participation as part of the team. In the case of some men, their participation as part of the team can sometimes be described as competitive rather than as equal participants within discussions or action items.

3. Respect: Without respect, empowerment cannot exist. If a person is not respected for their opinions, they cannot feel empowered. Respecting others can only come about if you are respected for your skills and contributions. Those men who do not respect others do not usually garner true respect. Instead, they are feared.

4. Compassion: Compassion is an important attribute because it allows the person to understand how others' lives are impacted by life situations. Therefore, compassion creates empathy for those in a less-fortunate position, either at work or in their personal lives. It is important to note that being compassionate and showing empathy becomes more difficult if you are treated less than fairly or equally in your work as well as in your personal life. Compassion tends to be less evident in men who are used to ruling with an "iron hand," as this is perceived to be a more feminine trait and, therefore, unacceptable.

5. Humility: Humility allows a person to understand that to truly be empowered you must know your limitations, the limitations of those around you, and, therefore, acknowledge that there are many who may contribute to the overall good of the team. Being humble is certainly different than acting subservient when discussing your ideas. In other words, acknowledging others doesn't mean that you have to allow them to plow over you. Men who believe they have an answer to everything will rarely display humility or acknowledge the contributions of others. They might allow other men to voice their opinions, but they themselves will remain the leader and in control during any discussions as often as they can, relegating others' opinions as inconsequential.

6. Calmness: Without staying calm, a person cannot feel empowered in the decisions that need to be made. However, staying calm can be a challenge when you are walking on eggshells around others who are constantly berating you or when you are in fear of your ideas being dismissed. Some men in positions of leadership may instead be described as having nerves of steel—staying cool, calm, and collected—under the worst of circumstances. Although they are able to demonstrate this trait with ease, they, unlike women, have the advantage of fewer challengers to their ideas. Those who do challenge them can be dealt with, again, by a raised voice or dominant body language.

7. Acknowledgment of Others: Just as in the case of humility, an acknowledgment of others demonstrates that others do not threaten your leadership. Certainly the need to acknowledge others becomes even more difficult when

there is little to no acknowledgment of your own work, ideas, or feelings, as can happen to many women working in a male-dominated environment, or, as I like to call it, "The Good Ol' Boys Club." In our society, men are not expected to acknowledge others. Those who are in positions of leadership can simply rule. Of course, not all men will behave this way, but it comes easier to them because it there is a societal standard that allows for this type of behavior.

8. Honesty: How important is honesty? Imagine a life without honesty. The mistake many people make is to equate empowerment with power. In reality, it is the lack of honesty that can more easily create the delusion of power. However, honesty only allows for empowerment to grow. This attribute seems less impacted by the inequities between men and women; however, in the desire to be accepted, honesty in both men and women is sometimes seriously compromised.

9. Courage: To be courageous allows the foundations of empowerment to be supported. Without courage, both men and women are likely to speak the truth, acknowledge others, and stay calm during troubled times—all important attributes of empowerment. Interestingly, being courageous is, in our current society, more often attributed to men. Women who are deemed courageous often are described as having "balls." However, courage can take many forms, including, most importantly, the ability to tell the truth in difficult situations. When power can be affected by truthfulness, we see that men might not be up to the task. For them, the desire for power may trump honesty.

10. Achieving Success: The attribute of wanting to achieve success becomes important to the creation of empowerment because without this desire, there would be a lack of impetus to be empowered in the first place. It's easy to understand why this isn't easily found in women. For women who are not in a good place in their lives, their sole concern might be survival, not becoming successful. Certainly, the level of what is considered a success by women—such as being heard and acknowledged—is most definitely a lower standard than what a man considers as success—winning an argument, taking over the boardroom, or climbing the corporate ladder.

11. Enjoyment: To enjoy your work as well as your personal life allows you the ability to be empowered in your decisions concerning both. Enjoyment can be particularly difficult for women to achieve if they work in situations where their ideas are discounted. For most men, whether they are truly empowered or just "in power," I believe that a feeling or belief of being in power equals the enjoyment of the fruits of their success. This definition is far removed from a woman's perspective of enjoying her work. When allowed, her enjoyment stems from her ability to positively affect others' lives and make a difference in the world.

I must state that, while these attributes haven't been formally researched as to what is needed to empower both men and women, we should challenge ourselves to examine these examples and seek additional attributes that are also meaningful. I truly believe that each of the attributes listed is a necessary quality for an empowered person to possess. I am, of course, emphasizing the role of these attributes to empower women because I believe we are lacking when it comes to possessing all of these. I also believe that although men possess some of these, others are misaligned in their execution and come off more like "power" attributes rather than true empowerment. However, keep an open mind and be aware of the preconceived notions you might have developed as a product of a male-dominated society.

After each fairy tale, I've included a description of a well-known person's life to demonstrate that each attribute isn't impossible to achieve. It's important to note that these attributes aren't make-believe; they aren't relegated to the fantasy world. These attributes are achievable by all women and men. While the task may not come easily—as it does in fairy tales—success at any level is always fraught with challenges. These challenges are even more pronounced for women struggling with empowerment in a "man's world." I strongly believe that all attributes must co-exist together to enable either a woman or a man to become empowered. Some attributes may be more evident or stronger than others; I've chosen to highlight each particular attribute separately for emphasis.

In the other examples, either from my own experience or those of my colleagues, you'll witness how women still have had to prove themselves through adversities—sometimes successfully and sometimes not.

As we examine the often-misguided approach men exhibit toward women in the workplace and at home, you'll probably recognize experiences similar to your own. You don't have to look too far to find inequities in work-related projects, compensation, or advancement.

Similarly, a woman's role at home—in terms of responsibilities, child rearing, and decision making—also continues to reflect dark-age thinking. As an example, I still frequently hear from fathers of brides, "How do I know my future son-in-law will be able to take care of my daughter and support her?" This sentiment is prevalent in our society, and its validity or absurdity is never questioned. It's simply taken as fact, so much so that I recently heard of a father who asked his future son-in-law for credit and health records to make sure he could take care of his daughter. Incredibly, the news reporter for this story questioned whether asking for such personal records was appropriate, but the absurdity of the sentiment behind the request itself was never questioned. In today's world, a woman is more than capable of taking care of herself—both financially and emotionally. This story further illustrates how ingrained these misconceptions of women's independence continue to be.

On a more serious note, physical and verbal abuse, domination, expected roles in the house, and lack of overall appreciation for what a woman does continue to plague us. As we will see later on, not even our Constitution protects us, despite the fact we are living in the 21st century.

In today's world, I believe women need tools they can use to better handle the mixed messages they constantly receive about who they are and how they should behave at work and in their personal lives. We must be able to teach our children (yes, I'm including boys—they also must learn about the equality of the sexes at an early age) that we all have equal say in our dreams and our ability to make those dreams a reality. We can start with fairy tales, but if you are a woman picking up this book to get advice and insight on evolving into your empowerment, I hope the real life examples will also inspire you.

At the end of each chapter, I've included a worksheet with questions to help guide you in your quest to empowerment. I also believe they're a great tool for helping your daughter develop the skills she'll need to successfully navigate through life.

Finally, I end the book with the "Ultimate Fairy Tale." This story will bring all the attributes together to illustrate the power achieved when women become empowered in the world. The happy ending in this story involves all of humanity.

So, let's begin.

Part I

The History of the Glass Ceiling

The term *glass ceiling* was first used by Marilyn Loden in a speech in 1977. It has been and continues to be used to describe an organization's invisible barriers that prevent women from rising to leadership positions.

Chapter One

Equality of the Sexes: What Equality Really Means

First, let's try to answer the questions, "Why have we, as women, had to struggle to be heard, seen, and listened to with respect? Why hasn't the concept of equality been natural to the development of mankind?"

The answer may actually surprise you.

Remarkably, the ancient world held a clear matriarchal bent in how society viewed women. Female deities were venerated, and the female form evoked fertility, prosperity, and comfort. As the world became more educated in the physical sciences, these concepts fell by the wayside and were replaced with a focus on the differences in human form between men and women, so much so that from the time of ancient Greece, we see the beginning biases against women starting to form.

It was during the period of ancient Greece that gender concepts were filtered through the lens of biomedical theory surrounding the human female anatomy. In essence, the female form was considered inferior. The belief was that the physical features of a female were defective because she had no visible external genitalia. Early Greeks compared her form to what they considered to be the perfect human form, the male. His genitalia were external and therefore visible to the naked eye (no pun intended); she was obviously less than perfect, and therefore cast as inferior. Here is where the concept of woman-as-subservient-to-man appears to have its beginning; it has continued to grow with each passing generation.

As we look further ahead in time, into the Renaissance era, the male form was the predominant human form used in the medical books. Even in the modern era, the male physique is considered the standard for teaching medicine. Physiological formulas that "adjust" for the female form are still being used, and male illustrations continue to outnumber female illustrations in modern medical textbooks.

In modern-day medicine, one of the disciplines, embryology—the study of fetal development—appears to inadvertently further support the idea that the male is superior to the female. The accompanying logic is that when the fetus is developing, it's asexual and has the ability to become male or female, depending on the hormonal influences on the fetus. If there is testosterone stimulation, the fetus becomes a male. If there is no testosterone, the fetus becomes a female. The argument goes that the dominant sex is the male because, with passive development, the fetus becomes a female. I believe I can turn this argument around to say that, because the male fetus requires a hormonal influence to become a male, it's a dependent organism. Therefore, the female fetus should be considered dominant because it needs no influence to become a female. This, to me, is a much more logical argument.

I don't understand why we, as women, didn't stop these faulty arguments from becoming the new truth back then. Why did we remain silent?

I'm not sure what the answer is—perhaps these thoughts slowly became indoctrinated into popular culture. Perhaps the power of creating life frightened men so much that they found reasons to label women as inferior. Perhaps, at that time in history, there was actually a role reversal where women were deemed powerful because they could give life and men couldn't. Because of this, men wanted our power. Because they couldn't procreate, they found power by putting us down in other ways. Instead, women's roles were limited to procreation (no longer considered a powerful distinction from men) and the maintenance of a home.

Unfortunately, early religious writings also helped to propagate the concept that the male was superior. Not surprisingly, it was male writers who said that male superiority was, in fact, a "God-given" right and therefore not to be argued with or denied. Disagreeing with this philosophy would be considered blasphemous, and those who would preach otherwise were labeled heretics—a crime that in some circles was punishable by death. As the artistic expression of religion developed, God continued to be depicted as a male figure. It's only recently that we have begun to imagine the Higher Source as unassociated with any sexual description.

Now that we have a better sense of how the concept of male superiority came about, we can turn our attention to the true definitions of the words "feminism" and "equality." To do this, we must first begin with word origins.

The English word "female" originally comes from the Latin word *femella*. However, the word we use today doesn't directly derive etymologically from this. The modern-day spelling was created as a parallel to "male" in the fourteenth century.

The English word "woman" is the combination of the Anglo-Saxon *wif* (female) and *man* (a human being). In a non-etymological sense, if we look at another language source—Hebrew—the word for woman *(isha)* is a derivative of the Hebrew word *ish,* and it literally translates as "from man."

In these cases, you can see that the woman or female comes after man—more as an afterthought than as a separate being. The origin of words, therefore, seems to set the stage for the ongoing thought processes that stem from the definition of these words, thereby perpetuating man over woman or woman originating from man. This is important—if we aren't clear about these definitions and word origins, the concepts associated with them can't be accurately understood.

Further descriptions can be found in Merriam-Webster's definition of feminism, where feminism is defined as, "a social movement that seeks equal rights for women." An alternative definition given says that feminism is "the theory of the political, economic, and social equality of the sexes."

By both these definitions, feminism is a concept that applies to all areas of life—socio-economic, political, and health-related issues as they pertain to each sex. Gender equality is part of what defines feminism.

In understanding the idea of gender equality, one of the clearest definitions is found at the beginning of the Enlightenment, at the turn of the eighteenth century. During this period, the philosopher Mary Wollstonecraft wrote in her *Vindication of the Rights of Women*:

> No one person has the natural right to suppress, silence or dominate any other person, simply because of where both are situated in society.

This idea has been adopted by many seeking gender equality. To this day, it continues to be a powerful political message around the globe, helping shape the politics of equality in all areas of life.

It becomes clear that gender equality—which is an integral part of feminism—is actually a fairly simple, uncomplicated concept. Complications arise, however, when cultural and historical beliefs cloud the definitions' true intent. When these biases are added to the mix, the concept of equality enters into murky waters. By understanding our collective history, however, we can better understand the direction we should take on our search now.

Incredibly, the Suffrage movement, which is considered the primary 19th century movement for equality of women, was influenced by the living examples of our Native American neighbors. For the most part, their tribes lived according to the same principle described by Mary Wollstonecraft. For example, Iroquois women had voting rights, and Seneca women had the right to initiate divorce proceedings when a marriage turned sour. It's ironic that the Native Americans—who were considered a barbaric people—were actually more civilized and enlightened based on how women were treated.

Initially, it was the early frontrunners of the Suffrage movement—including Alice Fletcher, Matilda Gage, and Francis Wright—who hailed Native American women's rights as examples of how society could benefit from equality. They then influenced others: Lucy Stone, Elizabeth Cady Stanton, Susan B. Anthony, Harriet Hunt, and Lucretia Mott. These women were the pioneers of the early women's rights movement. Lucy Stone famously linked these rights to anti-slavery. She eloquently declared that women were just like slaves, beholden to their masters (i.e., their husbands), unable to earn their own keep, or have a voice in the day-to-day decisions of their families. The Suffrage movement grew in numbers largely due to her lectures across the country. We most notably see her in Boston, where she—together with Elizabeth Cady Stanton—organized the 1848 Seneca Falls Convention.

This gathering called for full legal equality with men, including full educational opportunity and equal compensation. It gained in momentum up until the Fourteenth Amendment was passed, which granted full citizenship and equal protection under the law to former slaves, but did nothing to further the cause of gender equality. That's because the Fourteenth Amendment, as written by men, didn't address the rights of women.

The National Women's History Museum, ww.nwhm.org, cites that female abolitionists faced discrimination against women and began to see similarities between their situation and that of the slaves. When Elizabeth Stanton and Lucretia Mott attended the World Anti-Slavery Convention, held in London in 1840, they were denied seats because they were women. That's when they decided to hold their own Convention. They continued to fight for equality among races—anti-slavery—as well as women's rights. In fact, the initial Fourteenth Amendment was also supposed to include women's rights.

Why did the Fourteenth Amendment fail to address women's rights and only focus on anti-slavery? It was as if men couldn't bear to lose two battles. They had to choose between freeing the slaves or freeing women—who were essentially slaves. They couldn't seem to do both. In the minds of some men, the world was becoming unrecognizable.

Thankfully, the Suffrage movement continued the fight against inequality of the sexes and evolved as a political force as it sought to give women what the Fourteenth Amendment failed to—the right to vote. Voting rights were, at the time, a huge hurdle to overcome in order for women to be considered equal members of society. This goal was finally achieved when Congress passed the Nineteenth Amendment in 1919 and the states ratified it in 1920.

Despite this victory, other features of equality simply didn't—and couldn't—enter into the political discourse. After all, a woman still knew her place in the home. The protection assured her by the man of the house was still paramount. She knew she couldn't survive in the world without an education; since education wasn't a priority for women, the only right she could fight for without jeopardizing her ability to survive was the right to vote. Other rights would have to wait.

And so, eventually, the concept of full equality for women was put on the back burner until the mid-20th century. Post World War II women looked for more opportunities to be active outside of the home. During this time period, education for women became more accepted, and it translated to careers for many women—even if those were limited to a handful of vocational choices such as secretarial jobs, stenographers, sales clerks, and beauticians. As the availability of higher education for women gained traction, the equality movement grew into what was popularly known as Women's Lib.

One of the most visible leaders of this movement, Gloria Steinem, was a champion the ERA, the Equal Rights Amendment. Interestingly, women's rights were only part of what was emphasized in this amendment. The ERA incorporated the basic concept of equality among all—regardless of sex, sexual preference, creed, race, economic or educational status, physical appearance, or ability. Steinem's speech at the National Women's Political Caucus in 1971, "Address to the Women of America," delivered an important concept—humanism.

> *This is no simple reform. It really is a revolution. Sex and race, because they are easy and visible differences, have been the primary ways of organizing human beings into superior and*

inferior groups and into cheap labor, on which this system still depends. We are talking about a society in which there will be no roles other than those chosen or those earned. We are really talking about humanism.

Ms. Steinem, continues, even now, to play an active role in women issues and has expanded her involvement to other women's issues including genital mutilation, abortion, and same-sex marriage.

The unfortunate reality, however, is that despite the advancements we see today that have resulted from the hard work of so many—including Gloria Steinem—we are, sadly, still far behind at home and at work.

If we examine the U.S. Constitution, would it surprise you to find that there is no language specifically guaranteeing equal rights based on gender?

Remarkably, the Equal Rights Amendment was just three states short of the 38 states needed for ratification as part of the Constitution when it was voted on in 1982 (www.equalrightsamendment.org). There is hope, though. In March 2013, during the 113th Congress, the ERA was re-introduced. Our nation is seeing a resurgence of energy building up to push the ERA forward. Sisters, we need to take up the cause again. We can't allow the ratification to be unsuccessful again. Each time we fail, we lose more momentum for our cause and remain in an era of servitude with lower pay for the same jobs men do and lack of overall respect for our talents.

After all, it was a hard and long road these brave women took to pave the way toward equality. We can't let their sacrifice be in vain. Despite all the adversity they faced, they managed to survive and have their voices heard. While I believe these pioneers in women's rights would be proud of how far we've come, we still have much more to struggle with.

In essence, what started out as a simple plea for equality among the sexes has now taken on the more complicated stance of full equality for all of humanity.

Nowadays, modern social psychologists describe social behavior and gender differences in terms of promoting the self vs. promotion of the group. They talk about the differences between men and women's approaches and how these are manifested at work and in relationships. Women tend to be viewed as having more "communal" traits, which are described as dependent, nurturing, and submissive. Men, on the other hand, are more often viewed as having "agentic" traits, which show them to be strong, action-oriented, and independent. Even though, at first blush, these characteristics may seem like innocent descriptions of the "norm," the implication, of course, is that the agentic traits trump the communal traits, since the former represents personal power while the latter de-emphasizes the self. (*The Dynamics of Masculine-Agentic and Feminine-Communal Traits*, Abele, A. J. in, "Personality and Social Psychology," 2003, Vol. 85, No.4, 768-776).

My first question is why have these differences been structured as power versus weakness? After all, there really is nothing wrong with either of these traits. Together, they work beautifully, much like Yin and Yang. However, by putting labels on these traits and judging them, we have continued to place women in subservient roles. Sadly, we perceive the truth of these distinctions when we look at today's society, thereby creating a self-fulfilling prophecy.

We can easily gauge the value society places on these two types of traits by studying the careers associated with each. We actually find that the behaviors women are associated with—communal and nurturing—are more frequently associated with lower-paying careers such as social work, nursing, and childcare. However, technical career fields in which men outnumber women are, in fact, higher paid. I'll go into more detail on this subject when I spend time discussing each attribute.

Individuals who demonstrate traits in opposition to those associated with his or her gender are—more often than not—perceived unfavorably. For instance, a woman who demonstrates agentic traits is viewed as either too cold or aggressive; the man who shows more communal characteristics is seen as weak. The empowerment process means that each gender is allowed to use traits of both. The individual in whom these are combined is a whole person, capable of being strong yet compassionate.

Let's use the hypothetical situation below to explore how this plays out within many households across the country.

Imagine a two-career couple taking care of their baby. Both the husband and the wife are physicians, one at a hospital and the other in an office practice. Their child's caregiver for the day gets sick and is unable to come to the house to babysit while mom and dad go to work. What solution is usually taken to provide for childcare? I'm certain that the majority of times, if not always, the wife will call in sick to take care of their child, not the other way around. Why is this? Is the wife's job or career any less important? Are these decisions made by mutual agreement between both parents? Is it always the expectation that the wife sacrifices her career for her husband's?

Here's another scenario—this one actually happened.

Recently, I interviewed a woman for a research position at the hospital where I work. Her curriculum vitae and research credentials were impressive, yet she was only considered a research associate at her current job. I was shocked when she told me this. Had a male in her profession had the same CV, he would undoubtedly be the head of his department, tenured, and well respected. How is it that she was only considered a research associate?

Being in the throes of writing this book, I had to ask her why. She politely explained that she had followed her husband so he could take a position of full professorship in his department. The very fact that she followed him made her what is called a "trailing spouse." Despite her stellar credentials, she chose to follow her husband. Apparently, this isn't considered a respected move in academic circles. So, even with her remarkable research—some of which was groundbreaking—she wasn't considered to be as dedicated or serious as her husband.

It boggles the mind that, in today's society, such inequity still blatantly exists.

We are letting this inequality happen if we don't fight against it. When she was offered the position as research associate, she should have rejected it on the basis of her credentials. She should have fought for a better position. As equal partners, her husband could have assisted her by rejecting his offer of professorship unless his wife also received an offer that valued her credentials too.

Thankfully, the story doesn't end there. This woman later interviewed for a full-professorship position outside the state in which her husband was working. I asked her what would happen to him. She calmly said, "Well, he will just have to follow me, this time."

Although I applaud her for fighting for her rights, I'm saddened that it had to come to this, i.e., her husband having to move so his wife could also have the opportunity to fulfill her career.

Unfortunately, we must take extreme measures to halt this form of discrimination. As women, we must continue to stand for our equal rights. We must demonstrate that our careers hold equal value to the careers forged by our male counterparts—regardless of what that career choice is: professional or domestic.

Decisions about who's got the more important career can't be based on the gender of the person, or what that job description entails. It must be a mutual decision based on the importance of each person's work. If both are equally important, decisions need to honor both careers equally, even if that means one spouse moves for the benefit of the other spouse.

Employers also are responsible for not allowing such discriminations to be perpetuated. Whenever possible, they should equally see both spouses' careers for the value each has.

Of course, the definition of equality doesn't end at work. We must also be aware that the responsibilities at home should be equally shared and held in equal esteem. For many, this certainly continues to be an ongoing struggle. The perception that domestic work—always viewed as communal—is less important or menial has been deeply ingrained in our society. The inferior value that is assigned to a stay-at-home parent is difficult to break away from. We learn these roles from our parents who learned from theirs and so on. That is why it becomes critically important to change this archaic way of thinking with this generation, so that future generations have a different perspective.

As we consider gender roles in our personal lives, we may be able to make small changes that eventually will lead to a more global movement towards equality. We certainly can use the example of the early Native American communities where hunting, farming, and raising the children were all seen as equally important for the survival of the community. Another example of a group that values equality is the kibbutz in Israel; everyone's job is given equal importance.

The evolution of this concept would benefit society as a whole, not just women's equal rights. To be able to view feminine and masculine traits as equal in their importance would also go a long way to pave the road to gender equality. Gender equality supports human rights, as has been previously defined and actually seen in the two cultures just described. Imagine a world where this is the norm. It would mean that a parent's choice to stay home would never be seen as weak, but, instead, just as important as making a mark in the world—financial or otherwise.

Through these definitions and examples, we have come full circle—starting with equality for women and ending with basic human rights. We see that by preventing any group from being treated as inferior, we elevate the entire community to a place where everyone has equal rights. The ultimate benefit of this new reality would bring the world closer to the end of poverty, hunger, illiteracy, and war.

Chapter Two

*Progress for Women in the Field of Medicine
and the Corporate World*

The world recently celebrated the 100th anniversary of International Women's Day. What changes have we seen in the opportunities women have been afforded? What have we done to increase the freedoms that were hard-won by the women that came before us?

Let's take a look at two different professional worlds: medicine and the corporate world. Medicine is, of course, the one I'm most familiar with. The corporate world includes businesswomen and lawyers. Women who are in academic and research fields are also mostly within one of these two groups. I believe these fields make up a large part of the elite workforce.

Medicine

Historically, women who wanted to participate in medicine were allowed to be midwives and dwell in the homeopathic sciences. They weren't allowed to formally enter medical schools except in Italy, which, since medieval times, has allowed women to matriculate into medical studies without great difficulty. This, however, was the exception rather than the rule.

Here in the United States, it wasn't until 1849 that the first woman physician, Elizabeth Blackwell, graduated as a physician, some four hundred years after the first women doctors in Italy.

Unfortunately, history in some parts of the world, including the U.S., shows that women who wished to practice medicine had their efforts thwarted. Even today, the post medical school training of female physicians seems to be more concentrated in communal (and less agentic) fields such as pediatrics, obstetrics and gynecology, and family practice than in any of the surgical fields. I have personally witnessed a woman in a surgical subspecialty (remember, considered an agentic-trait career choice) being divorced by her husband, who was also a physician in an agentic subspecialty. What was the reason behind the divorce? He wanted a more nurturing, caring woman at his side, not one who was so "strong-willed."

This is an example of how labels and perceptions can adversely affect individuals. In this case, the female surgeon was one of the most caring, compassionate women I have ever met; she's living proof that agentic characteristics can co-exist with communal traits in the same person.

If we look at women in medicine, there have been changes and improvements—not to the extent we would hope for, but changes nonetheless. Certainly, many of us have experienced sexist attitudes to some degree, including being presented with "opportunities" to help us rise to leadership roles. But, if we look at the big picture, we are starting to see an increase in comparable promotion rates for women and men at many institutions around the country. Sadly, though perhaps not so shockingly, salaries for women still continue to lag behind.

One positive change is the significant increase in the number of female medical students in the United States. In fact, women currently make up about half of all medical students and residents.

This trend should eventually lead to increases in leadership positions both in the private sector of medical practices and in academic centers, but it's a trend we have yet to see in any great numbers.

The downside to the increase of women in medicine is that women faculty members still continue to earn less than their male counterparts in comparable positions. A 2004 study by Ash et al ("Compensation and Advancement of Women in Academic Medicine: Is there Equality?" Ash AS, Carr PL, Goldstein R, Friedman RH. *Ann Intern Med* 2004; 141:205-212) surveyed 1814 female medical school faculty members and showed them to have average base salaries that were $11,691 less than their male counterparts. Worse, sexual harassment is still highly prevalent; about 70 percent of female faculty in another study conducted in 2000 felt such harassment resulted in a negative impact on career advancement because such experiences can lead to low career satisfaction—as well as low self-esteem ("Faculty Perceptions of Gender Discrimination and Sexual Harassment in Academic Medicine." Carr PL, Ash AS, Friedman RH, et al. *Ann Intern Med* 2000; 132:889-896)

A recent editorial published in the journal *Obstetrics & Gynecology* affirmed that, "professions created by or predominately filled by women are uniformly under-respected including being under-respected in terms of political clout." ("Where Have All the Young Men Gone? Keeping Men in Obstetrics and Gynecology," Lyon DS. *Obstet Gynecol* Oct 1997; 90: 634-636) Again, we see the differences between the agentic (more important) career choice and the more communal (less respected) career choice creating an artificial environment where men are elevated over women in the field of medicine.

It's still shocking to me that in the twenty-first century these issues persist among professionals in a group where people are highly educated. How can this be? I can only theorize that the allure of perceived power dominates all thoughts of equity in the professional world.

As I researched these facts about the role women play in the world of medicine, I've come to the conclusion that the problem we face is actually threefold.

First off, there's a negative trend that I've noticed in some women who've made it into leadership positions. Some of these women—whom I've met in my travels, more often than not—don't possess the qualities that I believe help to foster today's up-and-coming female leaders. Quite the contrary, these women developed all the wrong attributes during their climb up the ladder. They were correctly considered bossy (see description below), showed no compassion toward anyone in a subordinate role to them, and, in general, were mean-spirited. They believed they needed to act in a masculine fashion to achieve success. They respected no one and definitely didn't work as team members, nor did they acknowledge anyone else's opinions. In the true sense, they were acting as bullies (one step above bossy). I want to emphasize, however, that I'm not against the use of masculine traits. I simply believe that positive leadership reflects a combination of communal and agentic behaviors. When this combination is used, bullies will no longer exist.

Recently, the word bossy has been considered taboo when describing women who are assertive. This is where I believe the attributes I list as important are being erroneously described. Think about it. Bossy entails someone who imposes his/her will on others. Being assertive entails, as I have already described, someone that takes into account all opinions or thoughts concerning a particular subject and then comes to a final conclusion. Therefore a "bossy woman" is one that tells others what to do, while an assertive woman considers all avenues and renders her decision based on the community thought. This is a vastly different description. My intention is for women to demonstrate assertiveness and be seen as such—not as bossy. Furthermore, my intention is for the difference between bossy and assertive to finally be understood.

Therefore, I believe attributes that combine both agentic and communal traits may help our young women succeed without having to resort to adopting the "culture of guyness" in the hopes of gaining respect and being listened to. I'll address later what we need to do when we come across women who are considered bullies because of their tendency to demonstrate more strongly their masculine—rather than feminine—traits. It is this imbalance that would lead many to call women bullies—and, indeed, they are. Let me be clear; I am not implying that being a male means you're a bully. Rather, if masculine traits are emphasized and not balanced with feminine traits, then, yes—you will be classified as a bully. So, the question becomes, "How do we respond to these bullies?"

At this point, I'll pause and share my personal story about working within the "culture of guyness." Early on, I bought into the fallacy that male characteristics were more desirable. When I was in medical school, I thought I had received the biggest compliment when I was called "one of the guys." In hindsight, knowing what I know now, I see that it was the biggest insult I could have received. Instead of being seen as a woman with my own set of strengths, I was lumped in with the guys and their male traits. As I've said, it's taken me a long time to distinguish between the two.

Now I realize why I should have rejected that comment as sexist. My learning curve has been slow. I'm also surprised that, given my experiences, I didn't continue this train of thought and turn out to be a bully within my profession. I don't know how I was able to identify and embrace the attributes of empowerment instead of bullying. Perhaps it was because, early on, I witnessed firsthand examples of women-in-medicine-gone-wrong, and I didn't want to be like them. They really scared me. I didn't like how they presented themselves to the world, and it frightened me to think that I could become that way. They demonstrated the opposite qualities of what I have always felt to be important in a respected, true leader.

Part of what inspired me to write this book was I wanted my sisters to become aware of these lessons quicker than I had so their achievements could be reached with more ease and in less time.

The second deficiency I've noticed was actually described in an article published in the *Journal of Women's Health* (Carnes M, Morrissey, C, Geller, S. "Women's Health and Women's Leadership in Academic Medicine: Hitting the Same Glass Ceiling," Volume 17, Number 9, 2008. 1453-1462). This article states, "Support for professional and personal work/life balance must become an institutional priority." What does this mean? It means that, in actuality, both men and women must be supported in their goals of juggling family and career. We can't discriminate against women who need more time, coverage, or leniency with project deadlines over men in the same position. Both men and women should be allowed to have both a fulfilled family life and a career, without one suffering over the other.

I read an interview with a female student who was in a study looking at how gender impacts the experiences of female medical students (Babaria P, Abedin S, Nunez-Smith M. "The Effect of Gender on the Clinical Clerkship Experiences of Female Medical Students: Results from a Qualitative Study" *Acad Med.* 2009 Jul; 84(7):859-866). In this interview, she described her quandary of being both a medical student and mother. She initially thought she could do anything she wanted to in terms of a physician specialty. She then came to feel differently about her medical career. Although she knew she'd graduate, she felt that her career choices were more limited as she went forward. At the time of the interview, her career choices had been determined by her kids and family rather than her interests. She no longer had the positive attitude that she could do anything she wanted. She was one of many who feel this way.

The study also suggests that the lack of support women in medicine receive sends the dire message that, if the glass ceiling remains unbroken, "...it erodes our nation's competitive edge in biomedical research, wastes considerable human capital, and prevents realization of optimal health and healthcare for everyone." In other words, if the current practices continue, we'll see a decline of family values and productivity. The act of attempting to break through that glass ceiling and achieve success is detrimental to women's families and their health. In the end, society as a whole is affected. In essence, we can't do it all and expect success in all areas. Something has to give. In the case of women, it's either the career or the family. We should never have to make that choice—for ourselves, for our families, or for society.

Third, in medicine, the common adages of, "Doctor, heal thyself," and, "First, do no harm," should be heeded. Too often, they're not.in our current world. When we see how the practice of medicine continues to devalue its female participants—both as patients and physicians—it's surprising that changes haven't occurred sooner.

Here's a true story that highlights how women are often treated as patients. As a prelude to this story, first ask yourselves, how many times have you heard of women being scorned in a physician's office for being emotionally unstable and not truly ill? They then walk out, only to be later diagnosed with a serious illness by a competent physician who listens rather than judges.

The story is as follows. A woman I know in the health profession recently had surgery on her foot. She was doing well for a few weeks, and then noticed her foot becoming more swollen and red. She was also having difficulty breathing and becoming short of breath with exertion, which she had not experienced before. She decided to get checked out at an urgent care facility near her house. After the physician—an obese male—did his exam, he told her her shortness of breath during exertion was because she was overweight, she was overexerting herself, and she needed to take it easy. He then sent her home. He did not seem to care that her shortness of breath was an acute event and that she had been getting around for six weeks following her surgery without any difficulties, despite her cast.

Thankfully, she had a good friend who went to check in on her at home later that evening. This friend found her almost unconscious and rushed her to the hospital. She was found to have a large bilateral pulmonary embolism and was admitted to the intensive care unit for aggressive treatment. She was in the ICU for two weeks. Had someone not checked on her, she wouldn't be alive today. All because a male physician thought she was overweight.

This is just one example that illustrates how the absurdity of male perceptions can jeopardize women's health. I can only hope that future generations of men and women, who have equal respect of both sexes, will make this scenario a thing of the past.

To recap, I see three prominent problems facing women in medicine today, both as professionals and as patients: women in leadership positions acting as bullies; lack of equality for men and women balancing careers and family life; and dismissal of women's symptoms as unimportant by male physicians. Isn't it time we address each of these issues to ensure a brighter future for our women physicians and patients?

First, let's tackle problem number one: How should we respond to women who are in leadership positions not because they have the attributes to empower them, but because they are essentially bullies? If we continue to allow them to behave in this way, we won't go far in changing trends.

We should challenge ourselves to take those first steps toward change. One way to do this is to model a different style of communication— I'll discuss these techniques in Part Two of this book. It also means standing up to women who act like bullies and not allow them to pressure anyone with their negative style of leadership.

I believe that women in leadership roles who lead through intimidation shouldn't be allowed to execute their negative style of communication in front of others. They should be publicly called on it through dismissal, public correction, or, if need be, ignoring their comments.

The following is an example of a woman—a supposed leader in her field—being called on her poor behavior. I was attending a national conference with a select group of doctors who were specialists in a certain area. During the open discussion, I explained about an innovative practice we were doing at our hospital. This woman physician, who was from an elite and well-known teaching hospital in the northeast, was the presenter prior to the discussion. She immediately cut me off and, in front of all the participants, began to criticize what we were doing at our hospital because it was not proven. She went on to say that she was doing clinical trials to test this same new treatment strategy we had initiated at our place.

It was very difficult to get a word in edgewise, but I was finally able to describe to the crowd that, not only had this practice already been shown to be safe in lab animals, but there was also another well-respected institution utilizing this form of therapy. Third, we were in the process of collecting data through an investigational review board, in preparation for publishing it. The audience immediately recognized that she continued to be unwilling to listen to my comments.

Thankfully, the moderator, who was also a woman, essentially stopped this woman from continuing to argue. Afterward, I was approached by many physicians, both men and women, who felt this woman acted very poorly and was so wrapped up in her own perceived glory that she was unwilling to listen to others. It was also clear to everyone that I had stolen her thunder and she was no longer in charge. The difference between her and me was that I was presenting to the audience a new innovative treatment strategy that might be useful to others involved with similar patients. She, on the other hand, wanted everyone to know that only an elite physician (herself) from an elite university hospital should be allowed to tell everyone else (not quite as elite as she) what to do. The woman moderator demonstrated to others her true leadership skills. She not only showed how to get her ideas across but also how to respectfully listen to others' ideas. Because of the moderator's leadership style, others were able to learn new ways of treating certain disease processes. Although she thanked this physician for her input, she nonetheless stopped her from making further comments and, instead, proceeded to ask others to continue to comment on their experiences.

This example illustrates how we are starting to understand the difference between thoughtful leadership and domineering behavior. There are enough of us who believe in the equal right of everyone to voice opinions, describe their successes, and help others learn a better way. As we see the new empowered woman emerge, the old guard will disappear. No one will want them to teach, or lead, nor will they listen to them pontificate about how great they are.

The second problem we face in medicine today—the lack of equity for men and women when it comes to balancing careers and personal lives—means that we need to promote those medical practices that support all physicians. The passage of the Family and Medical Leave Act in 1993 is a good start; it protects jobs for employees who need to take unpaid leave to care for themselves, newborn or adopted children, or next of kin who are ill or injured. Basically, it allows men and women to be present in their personal lives without risking their careers. However, this idea needs to transcend the law to become second nature; no one who has personal issues that require them to be away from work for an extended period should be singled out as less dedicated in their careers. They should be equally considered for promotions and salary increases, and, overall, valued for their contribution.

The third problem as described above—male physicians compromising women's healthcare because of dismissal of symptoms—can be addressed by redirecting those particular physicians toward appropriate diagnoses based on symptoms rather than perceptions. When we do that, they begin to listen and address the health concerns brought to them. If we cannot redirect these physicians, we must simply dismiss them as our primary or specialty care physicians and find doctors who will treat us as patients in need of help—not as hysterical women. If this trend happens enough times to a particular doctor, and the word gets around that he tends to assume women's problems are primarily psychological, his business will eventually suffer. He will learn the hard way.

All these examples, of course, pertain to medicine in the U.S. What about medicine and women in other parts of the world?

In other parts of the world, we do see a little more balance in the ratio of female-to-male medical students; in some countries, we find that there are equal numbers of both practicing medicine.

There is, however, an exception to the generally egalitarian approach to medicine in other parts of the world. There has been increasing criticism leveled at women in medicine in developed countries in Europe as well as in the U.S. This criticism centers on the fact that, despite the high cost of training for a career in medicine, women physicians have an increased tendency to work part-time, or even retire altogether, so they can raise a family. At issue is the need for medical schools to meet a quota of female students eligible to receive funding. The fear is that a talented male applicant—who might be viewed as more apt to remain full-time in his career—could be denied a spot in favor of a female. This argument implies that because we are allowing women to study medicine, we are creating a dire shortage of physicians available to treat the population adequately.

What no one seems to want to address or even think to address is how a medical career can also affect a male in terms of his participation in raising a family. In fact, despite the superficial quotas, the underlying social structure is still very skewed;

women continue to be seen as the primary caretakers of their families. They are unable to do it all—have a full career in medicine, have children, and be a wife and mother. Therefore, because they feel their families take priority, they abandon their careers. This might not be the case if there was true equity in the work schedule as well as work and family responsibilities. The real culprit isn't a faulty admission practice but rather an endemic imbalance in our personal lives.

The Associated Press wrote an article in 2013 that further highlighted this situation ("Pakistan's Medical Schools, Where the Women Rule.," April 19, 2013 by Rebecca Santana). In Pakistan's medical schools, women make up the vast majority of students. At first glance, you might be impressed that in a country that is trying to stifle women's education there are such significant numbers in higher education. However, further into the article the author relays that few of these women actually go on to practice after they graduate. Instead, their families encourage and demand that they marry, have families, and raise the children. Why, then, is there a push to go to medical school? Women with higher education are more desirable and have better prospects for marriage. So, of the 132,988 doctors who are registered as practitioners in Pakistan that actually practice, only 58,789 are women. Why do so few men enroll in medical school? It takes too long and they can make more money, faster, by going into business or IT careers.

We see, again, how the belief that women belong at home and not in careers is perpetuated in both underdeveloped and developed nations. Not only are we criticized for ignoring our families in favor of our careers, we're taking up valuable spots in medical schools meant for men and, therefore, cheating society of deserving male doctors. Instead of seeing the value women bring to society as a whole, we are again relegated to being second-class citizens whose role is solely home-based.

Corporate World

The statistics behind women in corporate America are equally disappointing. While there may be a slight, positive trend with a small uptick in the number of women leaders, the overall figures are still low.

The numbers show that women have been able to climb the corporate ladder but mostly only up to middle-management level jobs in support departments such as human resources and accounting. These positions, however, rarely lead to the CEO track. The top management positions, which are usually connected to sales and production, tend to be CEO incubators and continue to be poorly represented by women in the U.S. That is partly why, in 2010, only 2.4 percent of the U.S. Fortune 500 chief executives were female. (Forbes.com, "Disappointing Statistics, Positive Outlook," by Ginka Toegel 2/18/11)

Not long ago, I saw further evidence of women's weak influence in an ad I found in a newspaper. It announced the opportunity to register for "the #1 Business Seminar: Lead and Succeed 2013." All the speakers who were advertised to teach management skills, business skills, leadership skills, and more, were men. There was not a single woman speaker in the group. I was amazed, considering there exists a group—albeit a small one—of powerful women who would are influential speakers.

To me, this is an illustration of where we stand in the United States in validating women's expertise in the corporate world. In other words, we're standing in quicksand. The more we fight for our rights, the more we seem to be ignored and brushed away as non-contributory, until we eventually sink into oblivion.

Women's lack of access to the boardroom may explain why we are lacking in corporate leadership positions. Only 12.5 percent of U.S. boardroom seats are held by women. (Forbes.com, "Disappointing Statistics, Positive Outlook," by Ginka Toegel 2/18/11) What, then, is the "right" percentage, i.e., when women feel comfortable participating at the corporate level?

Interestingly, a study showed that when women comprise 25 percent of the membership in the boardroom, they are still considered a minority, whereas at 35 percent, the "tipping point" is achieved and visibility becomes relevant. (Forbes.com, "Disappointing Statistics, Positive Outlook," by Ginka Toegel 2/18/11)

If the number of women exceeds 35 percent, we become heard as individuals with our own set of ideas, no longer viewed as token women at the table. This means that women membership of over 35 percent in the boardroom allows a woman's views to no longer be linked to her gender.

Now, let's go back to what our statistics are here in the States. Well, with only 12.5 percent of seats in boardrooms occupied by women, we are nowhere near where we should be if we want to be heard with any authority.

If we look at Norway, a progressive country, the number of women in corporate leadership positions approaches 44 percent. (Forbes.com, "Disappointing Statistics, Positive Outlook," by Ginka Toegel 2/18/11) What is different about Norway? Certainly, this high percentage of female leadership did not happen by chance. In fact, what Norway did was to actively adopt legislation that required at least 40 percent of the board of publicly listed companies to be composed of women. This country essentially realized that women have valuable training and opinions, and make excellent leaders.

Unfortunately, what we find in Norway is more of an exception than the rule. The most recent statistics show that only about 5 percent of CEOs hired globally in 2012 were women, up from 3 percent over the previous three years, according to the global management consulting firm Booz & Company. It looks like Norway has a lot to teach the rest of the world.

If we consider traditional gender traits previously described—agentic (male) versus communal (female)—artificial as they may be, we see that when women become leaders, they are able to assimilate both sets of characteristics, unlike men, who retain agentic qualities and rarely display communal values. If, however, women attempt to only display the male set of values, they are perceived as insincere and less than authentic leaders. They are looked upon as bullies, a trait that isn't very attractive to women.

An example of a woman currently in a leadership position who uses both value sets—agentic and communal—is Indra Nooyi, the chief executive and chairwoman of PepsiCo. She has been known to make tough decisions by necessity. Yet, apparently, she is described as warm and caring by those who work with and for her. These are the role models we need to seek out and emulate. It's unfortunate that we have too few examples to showcase rather than too many.

What is also unfortunate is that the lists of women leaders from around the world may not demonstrate the true leadership skills described here. The world has yet to distinguish between women who are "little men" leaders and those that truly exemplify the attributes of empowered women and combine both the agentic and communal traits. I would venture to say that, in general, women in leadership positions who are "little men" are respected by most of the male population. Men often label these women in negative terms because they feel such women leaders can more appropriately handle the tough decisions precisely because of their male attributes. In general, men simply don't understand that using the empowerment attributes I describe rather than solely using masculine traits allows women to be effective leaders.

If you want to be able to distinguish between the two types of leaders, the woman leader who is feared is usually not an empowered leader. If that woman leader is instead respected for her knowledge, listening skills, compassion, honesty, and fairness, she is most likely an empowered leader.

Sadly, what we more commonly see is that the male traits dominate in women in leadership positions, despite the negative connotations, because, again, these are what men understand to be true leadership skills. The most recent example that comes to mind is Marissa Mayer, CEO of Yahoo, who reportedly banned her employees from being able to telecommunicate from home as part of their job. She believes this is not an efficient way to run a company—despite evidence demonstrating that among employees who are able to handle their personal life alongside work, both benefit and efficiency increases. Here we see, yet again, that what is being asked of others is that work must come first—an agentic trait. If you want to succeed in your company and climb the corporate ladder, you must give up the rest of what your life may demand. Agentic traits trump communal values in the corporate world to this day. My question is: At what cost to society does this reversal of values have? I daresay the cost will be high and may include an increase in divorce rates and children growing up with less than effective role models in emulating correct priorities.

So what's our outlook as women at present? Yes, women are slowly starting to achieve some levels of success in their professions and are becoming somewhat integrated, well-respected leaders. But, let's not delude ourselves—we have not completely arrived yet. In actuality, we have barely left the station.

We still have a long way to go, as I've described above, but at least the journey has started. My goal here is to make sure the journey doesn't get sidetracked or come to a complete stop. I want to avoid another failed attempt to amend the Constitution with a fully ratified Equal Rights Amendment; I want to avoid watching the work environment become more hostile toward women's equality. If these were to happen, we'd be scarcely better off than where we were prior to the Suffrage movement.

As I've said before, my hope is that the second part of this book will give you the skills necessary to help you achieve your own personal success story at work as well as in the home environment. Change begins with the individual. However, one lone person cannot make a big enough difference. It takes many to create the impact we need to affect change—change that empowers everyone equally and creates a world free of any type of prejudice.

Chapter Three

Progress for Women in Underdeveloped Countries

I begin this chapter by first talking about the United States. Even though we are, of course, a developed nation, we harbor a dirty little secret that affects hundreds of thousands of children yearly—most of them young girls. When we think about this problem, we typically think of the underdeveloped countries, especially Thailand, Cambodia, and Asia in general. Unfortunately, we must also recognize the same tragic problem exists right here in the U.S. and isn't well known by the majority of American citizens. I'm talking about sex trafficking and slavery or, as the United Nations calls it, "exploitation of underage girls."

The victims here in the U.S are abducted off the streets, held against their will, drugged, and then continuously raped so that they can more easily enter prostitution. The statistics are astounding and heartbreaking. Approximately 300,000 children a year are at risk for sexual exploitation (some believe this is an underestimation)—with most of these victims being girls. The average age of entry for children victimized by the sex trade is twelve years. Both statistics are per a recent U.S. Department of Justice report.

The majority of these children are our forgotten, discarded children; they are the children without any family to fall back on. These are the children of incarcerated and drug-dependent parents; the ability of these children to exit this lifestyle is close to nil. They did not make this their life choice; they were forced into it.

Many of these kids start off as runaways—2.8 million to be exact—because of the lack of family. A third of these runaways are then lured into the underground world of prostitution and pornography. These statistics are from the National Center for Missing and Exploited Children.

Remember, these are children—they don't choose to do this—and once in this underworld, they are physically and mentally abused. Attempts at escape are met with threats of harm to themselves, friends, or any remaining family members. They are true slaves. I was shocked and very saddened to discover these statistics. Our youth—our hidden treasures—are being squandered away every day right from under us and, in some instances, taken from venues you would never think of, such as the Super Bowl.

In the coming pages, I'll discuss the plight of young girls and women in underdeveloped countries. However, we should all be acutely aware of the significant problem we have right here in our own backyard.

As we look outward at the plight of women in developing countries, the hurdles they must overcome are even more significant to achieving leadership positions. This is especially true because education isn't even an option for women in many developing countries. As an example, women are still battling with exploitation and abuse in countries such as Algeria and Morocco, where two-thirds of these women are made to feel and, in fact, do believe that their abuse is justified As you can imagine, in these countries, education takes a second seat to basic survival.

More recently, the ouster of Hosni Mubarak and the advent of the Arab Spring in February 2011 placed the Islamist Muslim Brotherhood in power in Egypt. Unfortunately, their group notoriously views women according to fundamental Islamic traditions. These traditions, which we will further discuss in another chapter, relegate women to being caretakers and therefore give fathers permission to marry off their daughters at any age—even as young as nine years old. This, in essence, allows families to sell their daughters to rich men, securing their family's financial stability. They also continue to withhold women's rights in education and equal work opportunities.

To illustrate this further, in May of 2013, the Associated Press reported on the story of a male actor who posed as a conservatively dressed female. With hidden cameras, he walked on a busy shopping district in Cairo, hoping to shed light on the treatment of women in the Arab world. The hidden cameras were used to record the common practice of sexual harassment and abuse present in daily lives of women in Egypt.

This actor decided to do this investigation so that a conversation could begin about the abuse women still face in day-to-day life. He was motivated by the trend of worsening, violent, sexual harassment of women despite an increase in vigilante groups protecting women at gatherings. Although Egyptian law criminalizes assault, there are currently no laws against sexual harassment in public. Perversely, the comments after the documentary aired included the current conservative belief that women invite harassment and sexual abuse by mixing with men—not that men are the initiators. Therefore, the blame for the behavior witnessed in the film fully lies with the woman; she is the one who invites this harassment, not the other way around.

In 2006, the *Independent Review* published an article titled, "The Condition of Women in Developing and Developed Countries." In it, the author shares a global perspective on how women are treated. Below is a partial list of what women around the world deal with that completely eliminates any hope of having an equal voice in their society.

Denial of property rights: The hardships women face are exemplified by a practice that occurs in many African countries where farming is a family's main source of income. If a woman becomes widowed, her rights to the family land are immediately revoked.

In fact, women can only inherit land from their fathers if there are no male heirs. Even though they mostly are not allowed to own their own land, they are still required to carry water for irrigation, which many times can be far away. Of course, this chore is considered solely a woman's responsibility. If she becomes ill or weak, she might need to get water from a closer source, which in many instances may be either polluted or untreated. This, of course, can result in an increase of illness in her community.

Honor killing: This concept, though foreign to the Western world, is best described by a quote given by a brother who honor-killed his sister in Jordan and spent six months in jail as punishment. He said, "A girl is like a glass plate. Take a glass plate and throw it on the floor and it breaks. Would it be any use anymore or not? A girl is just like that. If she has been violated, she's finished." According to men who have these beliefs, that IS the end of the story.

Unfortunately, this practice is often tied to extremist Islamic law and therefore is also associated with the Muslim religion. For instance, in early 2005 in Pakistan, the government rejected a pro-woman bill that made honor killing illegal. Jordan followed suit. Turkey is only slightly better by imposing a life sentence to whoever commits an honor killing.

Dowry-related subjugation: In India, the practice of dowry extends to all socioeconomic groups. Even though the dowry is considered the woman's inheritance, she loses control of those assets once she marries.

In South Asia, dowry-related killings are a common occurrence. Suicides are also more common in women who may not have the necessary dowry to ensure a "good" marriage. In fact, in these countries, the expense of a dowry turns a son into an asset and a daughter into a liability—so much so, that there is a proliferation of female infanticide and sex-selective abortion.

Lack of legal protection: This actually is due to complete confusion between the differences in customary versus formal law in many countries around the world. Even though there may be laws to protect women, these women may be completely ignorant that these laws exist. They therefore continue to live under the vestiges of outdated practices, much to their detriment.

Exploitation of underage girls (sex trafficking/slavery: In many countries, marriage essentially ends any chance for continued education for women and therefore independence and continued economic liberation. The United Nations Children's Fund released a report in 2001 documenting the extreme situations in Nepal, where 7 percent of girls are married before the age of ten and 40 percent by age 15. One result of this is pregnancy-related death, making this a leading cause of mortality for girls ages 15–18.

Denial of education: While the Independent Review doesn't list denied education as an abuse, I'm adding it in response to all the recent killings of women and children seeking an education. We see this especially in parts of Pakistan and other countries where extremist Muslims have prohibited any girls or women to receive an education. If they attempt to do so, they are killed. There is the well-publicized case of the young girl who was shot in the face. Even more recently, there was a bombing of a bus taking girls and their women teachers to school. These extremists even followed the ambulances to the hospital, took the doctors and nurses as hostages, and suicide bombers entered the hospital attempting to finish the job they had started.

I'm constantly aghast at the terror women strike in the hearts of men who feel they are losing their power over women because of education. It's clear that is exactly why these disgusting murderers act in this fashion; killing innocents in the name of their god. They abhor the changes they see coming and will do anything to stop them so they remain in power.

After this long, lurid list of women abuses, the report concludes that the status of women is, in fact, associated with a country's level of stability. Thus, when women are subjugated, everyone is more likely to be subjugated. The oppression of one part of the population creates a climate in which the entire population can be oppressed. This is a sobering conclusion for all of us, in every country.

Let's look at other statistics that demonstrate the level of inequality experienced by women in other parts of the world. These were published by the United Nations in 2010. (The World's Women 2010: Trends and Statistics. United Nations Statistics Division)

1. There are approximately 57 million more men than women in the world. Even in nations that have higher populations, there continues to be a shortage of women.

2. Women are more likely to die from cardiovascular diseases around the world, including the Unites States. It's the leading cause of death in American women.

3. Although there has been overall improvement for women seeking and acquiring prenatal care, women in Sub-Saharan Africa have half of the world's maternal deaths.

4. Obesity rates in women are, on average, 35 percent in Panama and Mexico and, on average, 40 percent in Qatar and United Arab Emirates.

5. Globally, the rate of enrolled primary-school-aged girls increased to 86 percent in 2007. However, in Western Africa, the rates are under 60 percent. Another sobering fact that makes the above statistic even more dire is that the Women's Learning Partnership estimates that for every year beyond fourth grade that girls attend school, wages rise 20 percent, child deaths drop 10 percent, and family size drops 20 percent. Nations who do nothing to help their young girls get educated won't progress in the world economically nor will they become socially advanced. Their male leaders will continue to stay in power, which, unfortunately, appears to be what is most important to them.

6. Globally, women's wages still represent 70-90 percent of those of their male counterparts for the same work.

7. Job insecurity and lack of a social safety net is still prevalent in Africa and Asia.

8. Women are still rarely employed in jobs with status, power, and authority. In fact, in 2009, only fourteen women in the world held positions as heads of state or

positions in government. Of the 500 largest corporations in the world, only thirteen had a female CEO.

9. Maternity continues to be a source of employment discrimination around the world, despite the presence of maternity legislation in many countries.

10. Female genital mutilation still occurs, although the rate in Africa is slowing.

11. Women in rural sub-Saharan Africa are still in charge of water collection, which can take an average of over an hour a day. In these same households, solid fuels are used for cooking in open fires with no air circulation, disproportionately affecting the health of women in these areas.

12. The prevalence of violence on women and rates of HIV/AIDS is interrelated. Women who are beaten by their partners are 48 percent more likely to be infected with HIV/AIDS.

To counter these depressing statistics, the United Nations Entity for Gender Equality and the Empowerment of Women has published the following as the Women's Empowerment Principles:

1. Establish high-level corporate leadership equality.

2. Treat all women and men fairly at work; respect and support human rights and non-discrimination.

3. Ensure the health, safety, and well-being of all women and men workers.

4. Promote education, training, and professional development for women.

5. Implement enterprise development, supply chain, and marketing practices that empower women.

6. Promote equality through community initiatives and advocacy.

7. Measure and publicly report on progress to achieve gender equality.

These are the seven principles to empower the women of the world as presented by the United Nations. They sound so simple. Yet resistance to each one is embedded in the complexities of cultures and religions. The traditions that keep men in power and force women to be their personal servants aren't so easily replaced with more moderate ideas of equality. Change will come with great difficulty, and it will take many years, possibly decades, before a real difference is seen in the socioeconomic success of all the world's citizens. Health and freedom from abuse are fundamental human rights, not privileges for the few wealthy male citizens.

Furthermore, it's unfortunate that, to highlight the global plight of women's inequities as listed above, we need to resort to the commercialism of pop culture. The Chime for Change, a non-profit organization that promotes education, health, and leadership for women around the world, recently put together a concert to raise money and awareness of the challenges facing women today. This concert featured many big names from the entertainment industry with the hope that significant money could be raised. There was criticism about what these well-known women performers were wearing while attempting to sing about equality and empowerment for all women. Sadly, they resorted to dressing very provocatively. Their fashion statements did not match their stated intent. In other words, in my opinion and the opinion of many others, their credibility was definitely lost by the use of spiked heels, leather shorts, and thongs. It's already hard enough to get across the message that it's women's voices, opinions, and thoughts that are important—not their sexual prowess. Imagine how much more difficult it became to deliver this message dressed the way these performers were. Unfortunately, I believe they failed to get across the true message of equality. Yes, they did raise a significant amount of money, which will reach a large number of women in need of support—but at what cost? The money was raised because they highlighted their sexuality rather than their true talents. I'm disappointed that this mixed message was delivered to so many.

Please understand, I'm not a prude. Women deserve to enjoy and flaunt their bodies—but with dignity. Imagine if we turned the tables and men were the ones that had to express their need for equality. Imagine that, instead of delivering inspirational speeches, they paraded around in thong underwear to show off their masculinity. This wouldn't augment their credibility. The same concept applies to women.

Chapter Four

*How World Religions Demonize the Female Figure:
Past and Present*

Religions have played a key role in how women are viewed, valued, and accepted by their societies.

The difficult nature of this topic is that verification of a belief system is unattainable. Without any ability to corroborate what a particular religion promotes as "God-given" law, believers feel vindicated in whatever decisions they make in the name of God. As a result, concepts continue to be perpetuated even if their rationality borders on the absurd. Tales of man's superiority, written by male teachers and prophets and translated as such (perhaps incorrectly), become the convenient vessel, which continues to carry the traditions of women subjugation.

When we study descriptions of ancient civilizations, we see that ancient Egypt, Mesopotamia, India, and the surrounding cultures actually honored female deities. These societies were matriarchal, agricultural, and egalitarian, as well as peaceful. Around 4500 B.C., there was a shift, and a patriarchal, stratified, and, unfortunately, warlike culture emerged.

If we briefly examine each major world religion, we frequently find a troubled past and a conflicted present. Some more liberal factions of each religion seek to liberate women of the bonds placed on them from the past—a trend that continues today. Unfortunately, what I have described previously as the "glass ceiling" in the corporate world pales in comparison to the pervasiveness of the "stained-glass ceiling." In so many of today's religious groups, it is very difficult for women to attain leadership positions.

Before I continue my descriptions of each major religion, however, I'd like to share a personal disclaimer. I do not agree or disagree with the tenants of any of these religions. I'm merely describing what each of them preaches in their most fundamental, traditional forms, as well as their more modern versions. Again, I'm in no way endorsing or disrespecting anyone's belief system. I'm simply trying to state the facts. With that in mind, let's proceed.

Paganism/Wicca

Paganism is considered to be the first religion; it is the (generally polytheistic) worship of forces of nature. In the British Isles, women in the ancient pagan Celtic community become accomplished healers by using herbs and assisting childbirth as midwives. They were venerated by the community for these talents as well as acknowledged as leaders because of this.

Even as Christianity spread across the Western world, Paganism was not entirely lost; Wicca is its modern-day version. The Wicca community is now thriving in the States and around the world. It continues to honor the earth and use natural remedies for healing. Women and men are respected equally in daily life and in their religious ceremonies.

In fact, the witches of folklore and past history were nothing more than women who were demonized for their knowledge and talents in the art of healing. Unfortunately, the image of a green, long-nosed woman riding on a broom was created to conjure up fear. Men who were fearful of losing their power made these women into practitioners of evil. Hollywood continued to propagate this image because of its popularity. After all, evil sells just as well as sex.

When I visited Salem, Massachusetts, I found a definition for a witch that I've actually become quite partial to:

Witch: Woman in Total Control of Herself.

I believe that sums it up nicely. In fact, to my way of thinking, it would be a compliment to be labeled a witch.

Judaism

One of the first monotheistic religions of the world was Judaism. In the creation story in the book of Genesis, there are two accounts of the creation of man. In the first, more egalitarian version, God created man and woman in His image (Genesis 1:27). In the second version, God created woman from the rib of man (Genesis 2:18-22).

As we read further, the woman created for Adam, called Eve, then goes on to tempt Adam with the forbidden fruit. This act, which ultimately imperils him and eventually mankind for all time, results in them both being driven from the Garden of Eden. This is the groundwork being laid for the Judeo-Christian culture to emphasize the role women play in life. She is forevermore, in the minds of our religious forefathers, considered a temptress, not to be trusted, inherently evil, and only valuable as the producer of heirs.

More modern approaches to the Jewish faith have allowed women to serve as rabbis in the Reformed, Reconstructionist, and Conservative traditions.

Not all of Judaism allows this, however. There is still a great deal of inequality in the Orthodox tradition, in both religious and social laws.

For example, in Orthodox Judaism, the man is allowed to ask a woman for a divorce but not vice versa. So, if a woman is physically abused and asks for a divorce, the man is allowed to ignore her, move on with his life, and, in the process, leave her in limbo. She can't get re-married because she is seen as an *agunah:* a woman in limbo and an embarrassment to her community. The husband, although he is not allowed to remarry, can take another partner and have children who, in Orthodox Judaism, are not considered bastards.

Christianity

Christianity is an expansion of the Jewish faith and shares Jewish sacred texts. In Christianity, the sacrificial lamb that went by the name of Jesus, Son of God, came to earth to save us from the Original Sin of rebellion against God. This concept constantly reminds everyone that, thanks to the first woman, Eve, we were separated from God. I certainly do not want to insult any reader, but the fact remains that a core belief in Christianity is that a woman, Eve, got humanity into trouble; a man, Jesus, was sent to save us all.

In addition to the concept of original sin, New Testament writings also abound with the need for women to remain silent, subservient, and basically ignorant.

Another historical illustration comes from the famous library of Alexandria, supposedly full of the knowledge of centuries past. While it was in the process of completely being destroyed by fire a second time, Hypatia, who was the head of the Neoplatonic School of philosophy in Alexandria, attempted to save it. Instead of being assisted in her endeavors, she was dragged into the street by a Christian mob and killed, and her body was chopped into small pieces. She was targeted because she had once said, "To teach superstitions as truth is a most terrible thing." She was, after all, accomplished in mathematics and astronomy. A library, of course, was full of knowledge, knowledge that might be able to refute what the early Christians would consider truth. Therefore, any attempts to save it would be considered heresy. Later on, during Victorian times, her death was used as a lesson for women to understand the dangers of overstepping their ordained place in society.

German Inquisitors during the 15th and 16th centuries remarked that women were essentially stupid, had poor memories, and were unable to contain their sexual impulses. During that same time, tens of thousands of women were burned at the stake as witches.

The present day demonstrates only slightly better views of women; at least there are some Christian denominations that allow women to rise to leadership positions as ministers. The Catholic Church, however, has not changed its position on women's rights in this area. Although witches are no longer burned at the stake, little else has changed to indicate we, as women, are worth much more than being barefoot and pregnant in the kitchen. Contraception continues to be forbidden in Catholicism. It's as if a woman's role is only to procreate, not to also be allowed to enjoy sex. Celebration of our sexuality is taboo.

Islam

Unfortunately, Muslim scriptures, especially the Koran, clearly state that women are inferior beings physically, intellectually, and morally. A famous Islamic theologian, Ibn Al-Ghazzali, stated, "The most satisfying and final word on the matter is that marriage is a form of slavery. The woman is a man's slave and her duty therefore is absolute obedience to the husband in all that he asks of her as a person."

In the present day, statistics from the Women's Action Forum ("Report of the Commission of Inquiry for Women," 1997, Pakistan, p. 83) demonstrate the injustices that are still present. In Pakistan, 72 percent of all women in police custody are physically and sexually abused, and 75 percent of those women are in jail with charges of adultery, rape, or prostitution.

One bright change we see is in the emergence of more moderate leadership in Islam. Within mosques and study groups throughout moderate Islamic communities, the rise of strong Muslim female voices is beginning to be heard. They are teaching tolerance and the right of women to be educated. Unfortunately, today, women who continue to voice their opinions to strengthen other women are risking their lives constantly.

There are two recent incidents that serve as prime examples. One involves a Pakistani girl named Malala Yousafzai, the girl whom I mentioned earlier that was shot in the face as she stepped off a bus because she was a proponent of education for girls in Pakistan. Her attackers were almost able to silence her for her beliefs. Thankfully, she survived and vowed to continue to fight for the right to education for all women in Pakistan.

The second incident was the bus filled with girls and women teachers that was bombed. Unfortunately, many did not survive this attack. As you can see, much work still needs to be done. We have just begun and are a long way away from being finished and successful in our quest for equality.

Hinduism

The caste system certainly has not favored women in India either. Female infanticide was sanctioned from early times, through the holy Vedic writings of the Hindu. Young girls given in marriage could be abandoned at any time, and bride burning has been and continues be a horrifying practice in the present day, mostly in rural areas. This occurs so that more money can be extracted from the girl's parents. Accusations can come about for nothing more than being outspoken with men or priests.

In today's world, Hindu women are seeking liberation from the views of inferiority historically placed on them. However, they also face a long uphill battle in achieving social liberty and civil rights in all areas of their lives. Thankfully, the caste system is slowly being broken down, which helps afford women a better chance for equality. Much of the inspiration in the fight for equality initially came from their leader, Indira Ghandi, who strived to restore respect and honor for women of all means. However, there is a difference in how Hindu women see feminism. Their concept actually differs from the Western thought of feminism in that empowerment isn't yet what they seek. Instead, first and foremost, the removal of systemic oppression of the female population has become most important to their cause. They, in fact, have a longer road ahead of them if their final goal is women's empowerment. They must first fight to put an end to systemic oppression before they can work toward total equality.

Buddhism

During the lifetime of the Buddha, many rules and regulations were written for men. However, the number of these rules was significantly higher for women. After the Buddha died, Buddhism further became a patriarchal power structure, which held a view that women were obsessed with lust and sex rather than their religion. Therefore, in their religion, a woman could never be spiritually realized until she completely desired to become a man and, in fact, mentally became one.

The present day, however, has seen a resurgence of women leaders as dharma (religious) leaders, most probably because there isn't one agreement between the different writings or between the sects and schools. Therefore, in today's world, Buddhist women in the West consider sexism to be old remnants of an antiquated Asian culture, but the Buddhist women in the East are still struggling.

Baha'i Faith

Here is the last religion I want to describe. It's the second religion I found that respects women equally from its inception to present-day practice.

The Baha'i faith has always maintained that peace is only possible when women have achieved full equality across all areas. Since Baha'i was founded about one hundred and fifty years ago, it has been evident that women's equality has been and continues to be central to its message. There is no history of abuse, subjugation, or any form of inequity among the sexes. In every aspect of life, women are involved equally and fully. The most remarkable beliefs include the following: the feminine qualities that in the past have been classified by others as inferior are no longer so. These qualities include compassion, nurturing, cooperation, and empathy and are central to creating a peaceful world with prospects of advancing our civilization only for good outcomes. Baha'i is truly a model religion if one judges it through the lenses of equality, respect, compassion, and peace for all.

I presented the above brief descriptions of these major religions to give an important perspective on how women often have been relegated to serving men and have been deprived of the ability to espouse opinions or be considered as equals in any area of life.

After all, religious beliefs play a vital role in most cultures around the world and, in many ways, are difficult to distinguish from traditions passed on through the generations.

If there is little to no support in the consideration of women's equality by the leaders of the major religions of the world, how then can we as women begin to make any advances in any or all other areas of life?

That is why I felt this was an important aspect to present and discuss, so that there might be further clarity on the subject. I hope that the above descriptions of religions, in relation to women, will also help us understand better the challenges we face in our ongoing fight for equality. These challenges are certainly much more difficult than I had envisioned when I first started to write this book. Religion is a powerful force; when it is mixed with the culture and traditions of a society, the society's ability to bring about change will be much more difficult. Religion has the effect of voiding all possible common-sense discussions because, as I have mentioned previously, a belief system is just that: a belief. Arguments against a belief are not impossible because they are just that, beliefs, not anchored in fact.

It will take the slow acquisition of religious leaders who utilize scientific knowledge as another basis from which they can support their religious beliefs. In other words, radically speaking, education would actually strengthen a person's belief in a Higher Source, as well as encourage the spiritual side of science.

My hope is that these progressive thoughts, together with the realization that early writings were most likely merely an attempt by insecure men to garner power over women, might help begin to change how women are perceived by society as a whole. Once the religious/cultural barriers are taken down, we can begin to see progressive change toward equality for women in all areas of life throughout the world.

Chapter Five

Why Men Still Rule the World—for Now

Certainly, the previous chapter offers some insight concerning why, historically, men have believed (and, in some cultures, continue to vehemently believe and act on that belief) that they are the superior sex. If God has ordained it in their religious writings, it must be so. The statistics I have expounded upon in the previous chapters concerning leadership roles in medicine and the corporate world obviously demonstrate it's still a man's world. It's hard to give up all that power.

I suppose that the following questions, then, can be answered by the history I have presented concerning religions and cultures. However, I felt the need to ask them anyway. I also believe that, by putting these questions front and center, we can more clearly understand the answers and thereby have a better grip on how to counter the realities of the facts behind these answers.

These questions include:

1. Why do boys receive higher education in some parts of the world?
2. Why are health care allocations greater for male diseases than for women, even in developed countries?
3. Why is pay often higher for men than for women in the same job?
4. Why are women at a higher risk to become victims of violent crimes than men?
5. Why are women considered property in some parts of the world and treated as such?

6. Why are women passed over for leadership positions despite education that would otherwise qualify them?

7. Why, when women offer opinions, are they often called "bitches," but when men present their ideas, they are more likely to be seen as assertive go-getters who are displaying leadership qualities?

After our discussions in the previous chapters, I believe the answers are more readily and intuitively obtained. Between the facts I have presented, the U.N. reports available documenting the recent plight of women around the world, and the religious traditions that have and continue to propagate current values, I believe we have concrete reasons for the inequality we still see. Certainly, these reasons contribute to the prevalence of men in leadership positions. But again, why do these discrepancies still exist?

One would hope that in this century and in our current state of advanced technology, the old ways would be abandoned. The lure of power over others, however, is great. I believe that the obtainment of this power over others is, in part, embedded in age-old traditions and cultural barriers that can't begin to transcend the need for global equality. Religion puts the final stamp of approval on these traditions. The loss of this power would help hasten the changes we are trying to effect through empowerment of women around the world. Unfortunately, these changes, i.e., release of power and propagation of equality, will be difficult, at best, to achieve.

It will require significant education early in the development of young boys, which, in turn, will begin to show results only in the generations ahead. Then and only then will we begin to see women reap the benefits of this education, which will allow equality to become a reality. Even then, cultural blocks may continue to prove insurmountable in allowing for positive, progressive education.

It will take corporations to help change the environment at work, with policy changes within the corporation coming from the boards of these corporations. These boards will need to have committed people championing these changes for equality.

So, if these actions do not happen often enough to make change visible, are we doomed to a world where men continue to rule, with a few exceptions, as we see in today's society?

Perhaps the answer needs to start in microcosms of society rather than in the larger corporate world. Perhaps the answer starts with the family unit, as I've talked about above, with the education of the youngest members of the family all the way to the oldest member. This education starts with understanding the concepts of equality among the sexes at home as well as at work. It continues with the availability of formal education for all members of the family—boys and girls, women and men—and is of the utmost importance for the continued development of each member.

Although tradition and religion will continue to play an important part in each family's thought processes, the role of education will help temper these thoughts so that appreciation of the value of each individual becomes the norm and, in fact, is understood to be a crucial concept to implement. Then, as this family changes, it can start demonstrating new ways to function at home, in the work environment, and within its society and thus be a model for other families. At this point, these changes perhaps can become the norm rather than the oddity. As the community starts to see these changes, it too will incorporate them and shift toward equality. The changes then will create a ripple effect throughout societies until the changes we want—equality for all—become the norm and therefore the new reality.

I know this sounds very optimistic, but we have to start somewhere. Let us move forward with courage for our daughters and the generations to come.

Of course, it would be optimistic to think that starting with the family unit would be enough to help bring about these changes. We must also be able to see change concomitantly occur at the higher levels of society. For instance, governments could assist by placing individuals into leadership who are already empowered and willing to seek equality for all. These individuals, however, need to be voted for by their people, who want to see this change come about.

Unfortunately, power (or the perception of having power) is a very strong force in not allowing any of these changes to occur. That is because keeping a population uneducated makes it more likely that those who want to be in power will succeed. Thus, this becomes a vicious cycle that needs to be broken and one we see often resulting in revolution and civil war. Unfortunately, that is what may be needed in some countries, when the oppressed have had enough.

For change to come about, education needs to be available to a critical mass of the population. This education starts with the individuals and their families. Eventually, through education and modeling a different way, society as a whole would be able to shift from the concept of women's empowerment and equality to human empowerment and human equal rights.

Both men and women will need to look past gender discrimination. Mutual respect will beget mutual respect. Only then will we have come full circle from oppression to a liberated society.

Chapter Six

How and Why Little Girls Grow Up Un-Empowered:

A Pediatrician's Perspective

As I mentioned at the beginning of this book, I'm a pediatrician, mom, and wife—but not in that or any particular order. Each role is important, one isn't greater than another, and all enrich my life in different ways. Now I'm an author trying to convey to each of you how my life experiences have influenced my thoughts on the challenges women face every day, sprinkled with some historical and demographic facts.

If we are to begin to understand the development of gender bias, not from a historical perspective but from a developmental perspective, we must start at the beginning. A baby enters into this world within a family and society, with expectations already in place for that child. Remember that a newborn starts with a clean slate in terms of environmental influences, but the intrauterine environment does provide the first influences that the baby will experience physiologically. Although there are theories concerning cellular memories, wherein past life experiences populate humans from birth, we have no proof of this theory, so we must consider only that which we know to be fact. That is how medicine operates; anything else is no longer science and instead enters the realm of science fiction or fantasy.

Genetics is the initial influencing factor that affects a child and is critical to the development of each person. I always tease my husband and male friends that as females, we have XX chromosomes while, as I'm sure you know, a male's chromosomes are XY. If you take a good look at the Y, it's actually an X with a missing arm, which obviously means that a chunk of genetic material is missing. Don't you think that would explain a lot?

Seriously, though, these chromosomes do influence what hormonal factors will affect the fetus for life. Here are some facts, as we know them, concerning physiology, biology, endocrinology, and genetics:

1. Hormones play a role in fetal sex differentiation, in which the influence of testosterone creates male genitalia. The lack of testosterone in the developing fetus results in female genitalia. This all occurs around the sixth through twelfth week of gestation.

2. Sex hormones then continue to influence brain differentiation during the second trimester, where different parts of the brain are affected by these hormones (estrogen or testosterone) and thus develop in certain ways. This is independent of what is happening to the genitalia.

3. The result of these two separate processes during intrauterine development therefore indicates that brain development, in terms of masculinization or feminization, is independent of genital development and can lead to gender identity problems when puberty begins if there are abnormalities within either of these two processes. There are many ongoing studies concerning all of the above and, as you can imagine, the topic is very complex to comprehend.

4. We know that problems arise when there is an abnormality of either hormonal release or peripheral effect, so that although the brain becomes masculinized, the genitalia may not. Sometimes the reverse happens.

These complex clinical situations are what have brought this topic to the forefront. In the past, when we did not know about the brain being influenced in utero, babies with ambiguous genitalia (neither visibly a boy nor visibly a girl) were surgically made into girls, even though they were genetically male. Back then, the common statement among surgeons and endocrinologists was, "It is easier to make a hole than a pole." However, as these children developed, they had higher rates of suicide as well as significant gender-identification problems. At this point, it is important to note that homosexuality and/or transgender identity issues do not stem from abnormal hormonal influences; the above examples are clinical situations that have arisen and given researchers more information that would otherwise be unethical to examine in an artificial study. We still do not know why homosexuality or transgender issues occur. We do know, however, that both these situations are not a choice but rather a product of development, most likely during intrauterine development.

The above, then, is the biological explanation for gender differentiation and possible causes of gender identification issues, complex as they might be. However, these biological issues are less at the heart of the matter when it comes to girls feeling less than empowered. The confusion that exists, secondary to physical identity issues, overshadows any concerns about empowerment; in other words, empowerment isn't even considered when there are hormonal/physical problems that are being dealt with by the parents and the child. That's not to say that genetics, endocrinology, and biology have nothing to do with the development of empowerment later on; however, numerous factors influence how that a child develops into the adult behavior he or she later demonstrates. Those factors are very complex and perhaps as influential, if not more so, than the biology I just described.

These non-biological factors are, of course, the ones described in previous chapters: religion, cultural biases, socioeconomic levels, lack of education, and overall expectations that are set for that child by the particular set of parents or family members involved in the child's care.

Next, we need to refocus our discussion back on little girls and assume that the biological gender identification issues play a small role. That leaves us with environmental issues, which can contribute to growing up un-empowered. As I mentioned in the introduction, the brain is heavily influenced during neuronal development by the constant environmental messages affecting perception.

Therefore, consider the impact on a child who hears a constant litany of the following: "You aren't important enough, you need to find a husband, you're not good enough for math or science or higher education, if you dress like that, you're asking for trouble."

Here are some of my other favorites:

"Why can't you be as smart as your brother?"

"Why can't you be as pretty as your sister?"

"You need to be seen and not heard."

"Why do you want to work so hard at school? Just find a rich husband to take care of you."

These are all statements made by parents and other role models, who believe they are saying the right things to their daughters to inspire the correct behavior. Yet none of them realize how powerful these words can be to their daughters. These words have the ability to chart a course for self-deprecation and inadvertent failure secondary to ingrained beliefs of inferiority. They allow the brain to understand these statements as truth and reality. These are the faulty pillars upon which a personality develops and creates a self-fulfilling prophecy, as we have discussed.

If we focus on the growth and development of boys, we see similar verbal cues at play, only geared towards masculine empowerment—for instance:

1. "You can be anything you want,"
2. "You need to assert yourself in the classroom, in the gym, in the field, with your friends."
3. "Don't stand down to anyone, you are in command."
4. "Don't act like a sissy."
5. "Crying is for girls."
6. "You have the world by the balls." (As if the world is a masculine entity to reign in!)

These are just some of the statements also commonly used by parents, teachers, and coaches, directed at boys. These words are powerful, albeit engendering masculine power, for boys growing up.

As to why this happens, we must return to the discussions involving the particular culture in which each family lives. Therefore, breaking this cycle becomes harder than physically changing the sex of a person. The emotional strain placed on young girls to behave a certain way goes on to reflect on that society in terms of the successful leaders in place. Are the numbers of women and men leaders equal? Are salaries comparable? These are just a few of the markers that indicate equity exists within that society.

Even in developed countries, such as the U.S., the statements listed above are often heard in homes, in public, in the media, and in schools. Pop culture—in the form of magazines, ads, music videos, TV shows, and movies—often shows women in lingerie, playing up the sexual prowess of a woman as her most important asset.

So the question again becomes, *How can we change this?* Well, through education, starting perhaps with parenting classes. Also, pediatricians must begin to address these inequities with the parents or primary caretakers of their patients. As these parents/caretakers start modeling a new, more encouraging communication style with their children, we might actually see positive changes occur.

The public domain is another powerful force to begin to effect change. We are starting to see this in ads that show, for example, dads taking the kids to school. However, we need to see an overwhelming outpouring of women's empowerment qualities in movies, on television, and in magazines. When we start seeing more of these positive messages about the varied qualities women have—qualities unrelated to how they look but instead related to how they think—we will see overall society change toward understanding that we all have opinions and thoughts to offer.

As physicians, we also need to ensure that our medical schools and subsequent training programs not only teach students the above but also we must walk the talk, so to speak, in terms of our treatment of students and residents. Both male and female students should have equal time to spend with their families, and all areas of training must be open to everyone. Segregating specialties to being male- or female-driven should become a thing of the past. There is no reason females can't do well in areas such as surgery; women in those specialties should not be an oddity.

By helping to propagate this new thinking, we can begin to effect change and open doors for women, not only through our counseling of parents but also through our own demonstration of equity within our institutions.

As we move onward to the second part of this book, which I hope will help you make those first steps toward empowerment a reality, let's first relate the original fairy tale, so you can better understand what the chapters ahead will tackle. We must first describe the problem before we can start finding the solutions.

Remember: you will help lead the current generation into the future by your example, through your children. Imagine the changes you might be able to effect in the world through your example and through your leadership. Imagine a world without oppression, without the sense that power is the almighty force that leads to immortality. Imagine that, by providing equality to each individual, we can help eliminate hunger, decrease sickness, and finally see the decline of wars around the world.

Let's begin to become empowered for us and for our future generations.

Part II

Chapter Seven

The Original Fairy Tale (Nightmare)

Once upon a time—actually from the distant past all the way through to present day, in each generation—there lived a young girl born to a family of little means. Had she been born to wealthy parents, her story probably would not be much different from that of her poorer cousins, because all the girls in this land lived the same fairy tale nightmare. There was no escape.

Her land was constantly plagued with wars and forever ruled by men who wanted to remain in power at all costs. Their iron grip prevented education from being available to the masses, because the leaders feared that knowledge would render them powerless. As a matter of fact, only the boys were allowed to go to school, because girls were seen as weak in body and mind and generally unfit to think for themselves, let alone have opinions or solutions for the problems at hand. Why should money be spent on educating the weaker sex if nothing good would come of it?

In this land, girls had no opportunity to learn new things, to consider a future other than becoming a wife and mother, or to prove to others they were capable of anything but the lot given to them. Their confinement became a life-long prison sentence that left little hope for expressing new ideas or opinions. A self-fulfilling prophecy was propagated: this lack of education prevented women from thinking clearly for themselves, which ultimately appeared to prove their overall inferiority.

The women of this land realized that outer beauty was the only thing valued by others—especially men—so they grew up attempting to become more beautiful each day in order to gain more worth. They believed that this artificial value gave them an elevated status among the men, and so they would be less likely to be rejected outright simply for being female. As outer beauty became more important than inner beauty, they too became corrupt in thought and action as their priorities centered on acquisition of more material things to prove their worthiness. Humility, charity, and respect for themselves and others all were lost in this new materialistic world.

As the men of this land continued to rule, the laws became even more corrupt, and power was equated with social status, which served to further segregate others who were different, so that the uniqueness of each individual was lost rather than celebrated. Because of the corrupt laws, gradually a lack of honesty and ethics as well as a lack of compassion for other living things became the norm. Aggressive behavior became a standard response, and any acknowledgment of others' rights or opinions was viewed as weakness rather than strength.

A few radical women attempted to educate themselves and their daughters, but their efforts were met with violent backlashes. The fear this response generated only served to further restrict their access to individual growth and development.

As the wars continued, the land slowly became depleted of natural resources and could no longer support the population that depended upon it for survival. Sickness and early death became more prevalent, except among the wealthiest or most powerful. The work force diminished and the economy sank into disrepair, until survival of the fittest was the expected outcome.

Finally, instead of socioeconomic and technological growth to improve the land and create a better life for all, the opposite happened.

The ending of this fairy tale nightmare isn't a "happily ever after." On the contrary, the ending is sadly the destruction of all that was good, with progress coming to a halt and death claiming the final victory.

I know this is a very sad story, one without heroes or heroines. However, can you see the similarities between this story and the headline news you constantly are exposed to? Can you see the progression of power-hungry men destroying their respective societies to maintain their power over all? Can you see the lies that are propagated by these same men so they can retain their power at all costs? Lies such as these:

1. "I did not have sex with that woman."
2. "The reason education is suffering is because women work."
3. "I didn't rape her; it was consensual sex."
4. "She got me so mad, I lost control and beat her. She caused her own beating."

These are but a few of the many examples that can be heard coming from our leaders, pop stars, athletes—men who are supposed to be role models for our youth.

Can you see that if we do not stop this, we too will fail and move inexorably closer to the sad ending of the fairy tale nightmare? Let's continue on our quest to change this story drastically, once and for all, for the advancement of society as a whole and the final attainment of peace, overall health, and happiness for all the citizens of this world from this point forward.

Let's celebrate individuality. Let's make a new reality. Stay tuned for the Ultimate Fairy Tale at the end of the book to see how we can make this happen if we are given equity through education and respect. Together we can reverse the destruction that can occur and instead allow the creation of a better life and, therefore, a better world for all.

In the following section, I list the eleven attributes that will empower us as women in our lives, both at home and at work. Please take heed of the importance of this information. We are at a crossroads in our civilization. Women can't afford to lose their rights as equal human beings. We have much to contribute to the betterment of humankind, and our voices should be heard clearly and without fear of emotional, financial, or social retribution.

Our history brought us to the place we are today. As women, our fairytale "happy ending" is still just a fantasy. The middle ground is where we need to head, so that we can begin to achieve full rights.

It is my hope that the attributes described in the following chapter will get us on the road to this middle ground and launch us into a world full of equal opportunities, respect, and the achievement of that Ultimate Fairy Tale.

Part III

Chapter Eight

The Eleven Attributes of Empowered Women

Part I of this book covered history, definitions, and the influences that have created the perceptions of women as inferior, as well as the global perspective on women's rights. In Part II, I related the Original Fairy Tale Nightmare. In this section, you will see a different bent. Here we look at the proactive attributes that can truly bring about success in showing your community and the world what women are capable of.

Before we go further, I want to explain the significance of the number eleven. Eleven has been a sacred number since before the time of Aristotle. It's considered to signify the visionary ideals that we strive to attain. I don't think it is a coincidence that I have described eleven attributes that I believe are important to empower you as a woman, as well as an important member of society. My hope is that these eleven attributes will be the visionary ideals that elevate you to a higher plane and purpose.

As I mentioned before, each of the following eleven chapters starts off with a fairy tale character that has the attribute being discussed. An alternate ending of the fairy tale is presented to highlight the importance of that attribute. Each chapter then continues with the description of a well-known, modern-day woman who also has or had the same attribute. I then describe how a modern-day woman without that particular attribute (or with the opposite attribute) would look and act.

Personal stories in each chapter illustrate what can happen when that particular attribute isn't present—to further drive the point home. After these examples, I provide pertinent, relevant advice that I believe can help you to develop each attribute within yourself.

I end each chapter with a worksheet that should enable you to develop some firsthand skills to build that particular attribute for yourself. This worksheet will assist you to be able to use the attribute throughout your life. In these worksheets, there are no right answers—just your answers. You will know what is right for you. The only requirement is that you take time to examine each question carefully and answer honestly. Again, these exercises are meant to assist you in achieving the final goal of becoming a truly empowered woman in all aspects of your life.

Just remember: change is difficult and will require a lot of work. Breaking centuries-old barriers will result in your meeting resistance from others. Persevere—the results will amaze you, and you will be a better person for achieving this goal.

Before we continue, there is one last note about the fairy tales. You will find that the evil characters in these stories all seem to be women, and you might wonder why. Interestingly, until the last two centuries, male writers dominated literature, and you can often see a common thread or pattern in these narratives. Women were not allowed to write—after all, who would want to publish their works, since their opinions were completely disregarded as irrelevant at best and works of the devil at worst?

Therefore, we see that male characters evolved as complex and multidimensional, because men wrote them as such. These male writers, however, often relegated the female characters to two types. First was the good girl: quiet, humble, innocent, and usually a damsel in distress who was in need of a male savior—Prince Charming. The second type was the evil character: always plotting revenge, sinister, and many times also portrayed as a femme fatale. But was she really all of those things? Or was she simply portrayed that way to warn the reader that if a woman had an opinion, she would pay dearly for it? Remember, men were the creators of these characters.

Looking at these descriptions more closely, you will find that the so-called evil woman was actually the woman in the story who didn't stay silent. She had an opinion, a voice, and she told it the way it was. Were her thoughts evil and did she intend to bring harm to others? Perhaps she did, but the better question to ask is *why?* Were her intentions misunderstood? Perhaps the development of her character was such that by making her more verbal, she was made to have evil intent—after all, only good girls are quiet and obey the rules.

As a further example, let's look at the Broadway hit *Wicked,* the story of Oz's Wicked Witch of the West. Here, the role reversals between the good witch and the bad witch are remarkable. For the first time, we see how the evil portrayed was an illusion and the true evil came from the "good" witch who was seeking power. The song, "Defying Gravity," could be better titled, "Defying the System and Making Sure the Truth Is Heard."

In attempting to view these fairy tales a little differently, I have concentrated only on the good girls, teasing out more than the original characteristics that were ascribed to them. I have intentionally left the evil characters out of my discussions because their portrayal as such seems to have been intended to emphasize the evils of opinionated, vocal women who did not fit the image of subservience.

To put these misperceptions about fairy tale characters finally to rest, I would like us to start thinking more in the following terms: understanding that perhaps the evil female characters were nothing more than women who lacked the attributes needed to make them strong, empowered women but who wanted to be heard. Unfortunately, in their zeal to be heard, they came across as bullies, resorting to more masculine, aggressive, agentic traits rather than the combination of agentic and communal traits we would hope to see in empowered women. Since these characters displayed solely male traits, it was a given that they had to be defined as evil. Remember, possessing knowledge, having an opinion, and daring to voice that opinion were traits considered to be evil in women—the work of the devil.

Where the real deception occurs is when we look superficially at how the "good girls" were portrayed. They were quiet and simple-minded, with a single goal: to find their prince. Their "happily ever after" involved being saved by a man who would then take care of all their needs forever. These women did not need to have a voice, because being pretty was good enough. When women's rights groups have examined these stories at this simplistic level, they have rightly criticized them for their negative influence on young girls. Their concern is understandable when these stories emphasize to girls that all there is to life is being pretty and keeping your mouth shut, and that when you do this, you will find a man to take care of you.

That is why I have tried to reverse this negative perception through describing these characters differently and showcasing their more complex traits. Indeed, these characters have attributes that are worth highlighting and talking about, as you will see. In doing so, perhaps we can save these fairy tales from demise when women use them as valuable teaching tools to empower themselves and their daughters.

Enjoy!

Chapter Nine

Attribute #1: Exude Confidence

The Fairy Tale Version

Once upon a time, in a land far away, there lived a young girl who was described by the villagers as brave and self-reliant. Her courage, intelligence, and determination helped her through her adventures. When a war broke out that jeopardized her people, she did not want her elderly father to have to join the army and risk his life in battle simply because he was the only male in the house. She took his place in the army by dressing as a young boy, a deception that allowed her to fight and help ensure the safety of her people.

Despite the necessity of dressing like a man, the girl demonstrated the confidence needed to face adversity and negative impressions stemming from being female. You might think, "What kind of inspirational story is this? After all, she could not demonstrate that a woman was equally capable of fighting to protect her homeland." However, she first had to break the stereotype imposed by her people, which she knew she could not do by simply going out to join the fight. She never would have been allowed to fight as a girl. Eventually, when she returned victorious, she was able to declare who she was, at which point everyone realized the truth: her strength came not from being a man, but from being a valiant, courageous person.

Through her confident actions, she showed others that her gender had nothing to do with her ability to make a difference.

This is a powerful message for our young daughters about what their true abilities are. It actually highlights that they do not need to hide behind the guise of a man in our world to demonstrate their internal and external strengths; i.e., they do not have to use the agentic traits as previously described to make their point. Here is our first lesson about how, through this attribute of confidence, we can begin to be heard with respect and without resorting to being compared to a man. I believe this is a fabulous story to incorporate into our library of empowered women, if it's told correctly.

What if we had built an alternate version of the story? What if this young lady decided that she couldn't do anything because she was a girl, thereby allowing her elderly father to be recruited into the army? More than likely, her father would have been killed and, because the girl couldn't provide her strength and cunning to the army, the battle would have been lost.

Therefore, the story would have a tragic ending, not only in the loss of her father but also in the invasion and overthrowing of her people by enemies. There would be no role model to teach other women her attribute of confidence; in fact, the reverse would have been emphasized—that without the man's agentic trait of aggression, the people could not be saved. A valuable lesson would have been lost.

The Modern Era Empowered Woman

I believe that one of the foremost modern women whose name is synonymous with confidence is Condoleezza Rice, former U.S. Secretary of State, accomplished pianist, negotiator, and inspiration to women everywhere. She has served in both the private and public sectors with quiet strength, never raising her voice but with incredible determination in her words and body language. Her best-known role as Secretary of State demonstrated her ability to initiate many diplomatic efforts around the world. Her leadership has been influenced by the confidence in her decisions she has brought to the world table.

As with all the women I will subsequently describe, much criticism has been lobbied at Rice, mainly for her political stance during the Iraqi war. She was able to weather the criticism and continue to do her job—not only effectively but with grace. Condoleezza Rice, to this day, continues to be a role model to women who want to achieve a high level of confidence in their daily decision-making. She especially demonstrated that she did not need to dress or act in a masculine way to highlight her ability as a leader. On the contrary, Rice was mostly soft-spoken and dressed professionally, but with femininity. She had the ability to look others in the eyes directly and speak her piece with confidence.

Again, I truly believe there isn't a better role model in the public eye today for the attribute of confidence than Condoleezza Rice.

The Antithesis

A modern-day woman who demonstrated the opposite of confidence might come across as aggressive. For example, she would be harsh in her dealings with her board if she was in the corporate world, or perhaps bark out orders if she was a surgeon in the operating room. She would be seen as a bully in her communication style at her workplace or at home. Although there aren't many examples of male abuse by female partners, it does happen, and it would be considered an extreme example of a woman acting aggressively rather than with confidence.

My Experience

When I was a new attending physician, fresh out of my specialty training, I was taking care of one particular patient who needed a surgical consult because of his impaired gut function. I therefore consulted one of the surgeons on service we used. This particular surgeon, a man, came to see my patient and felt comfortable with the patient's exam, believing he only warranted careful watching over. However, as in all things in medicine, a patient's condition can change quickly, which is exactly what happened. I called the surgeon to update him on the change and my concern regarding the turn of events. What I heard on the other end of the phone line shocked me and was my first real indication, as a professional, that I had invaded a man's world—a place where I obviously did not belong, according to him.

His exact words to me were, "Don't worry your pretty little head over this."

Can you imagine if he had said the same thing to one of my male partners, even if they were junior? What do you think the response would have been from another man? I can only imagine the expletives that would have been heard. However, as you all know, he would never have said such a thing to a male physician. It would never have crossed his mind to do so, yet he felt justified in talking that way to me.

I was not intimidated, however, by what he said to me. I calmly responded, "You are simply the consultant and I'm the attending in charge of this patient's well-being. If you aren't concerned with what I have just explained to you, I will find another surgeon in town who will be more concerned and who will see this patient for me."

At that moment, he quickly changed his tune and apologized to me for this exchange. From that point forward this particular surgeon never disrespected me again.

More recently, in fact, twenty-five years later, I had another experience that was quite similar, but with a different male physician. After one of my patients was brought back from surgery, the patient's temperature was significantly low, which can impede heart rate, perfusion, and overall ability to recover quickly. As our team was recovering this patient, one of the male physicians involved with the surgery, who was sitting away from the patient and chatting on his cell phone, called out, "Are you all happy with your patient?"

I answered with the truth: "No, I am not happy." I said it clearly, not angrily, but with confidence. He got up, came over, and asked why. I explained to him that the patient was unnecessarily cold and required some extra attention because of this, but that we had the situation under control.

I then got called over to another bedside. This particular doctor followed me and, in a loud voice and in front of other staff, said, "You are a very rude person. Why are you so rude?"

In a calm voice, I told him I was not rude and that his perception was incorrect. I was simply answering his previous question as to whether I was happy or not. He was totally deflated and walked away, incredulous that someone would not quiver under his authoritative voice. I will no longer be intimidated by anyone who feels he can exert his perceived power over me. Had I been one of his male colleagues, he would never have talked to me in such an accusatory way, yet he seemed to feel righteous in his behavior.

Unlike the first case, and knowing this doctor's personality, I don't believe he will ever change his demeanor toward women. For him, we truly represent the weaker sex and require someone to save us. In his mind, when we do speak up clearly and with confidence—demonstrating our empowered abilities—he loses the opportunity to hold any power over us. His angry, public rant came from his belief that he had lost that power. Quite frankly, he never had it—it was all an illusion propagated by others, both male and female, who did nothing to stop his nasty behavior.

My Advice

So, what do my stories illustrate? What are the ways that we, as women, can show confidence in the workplace?

Certainly, our posture, attitude, and speech are critical. Dress also can be important, but that will depend on your workplace. Obviously, if you work in a warehouse, you will be dressing differently than if you work in an office or in a hospital setting. In any situation, cleanliness and having the appearance that you care about how you look will say volumes about how you perceive your own value. That, in turn, will affect how you are perceived.

For women, one of the more important points to consider in deciding how to dress is ensuring that you aren't intentionally provocative. Dressing in a provocative manner can send the message to your colleagues that you aren't serious about your work, or that being sexy trumps using your brains. You will not be respected.

A clear example of this happened just recently. A group of professional cheerleaders filed grievances about their pay, stating they were required to appear at functions and were not paid for doing so. The news commentator—a woman—then stated, "Why should they complain? Did you see how skimpily they dressed?" I was shocked that another woman would have commented on the fairness of the complaint based on the dress of the women complaining. This simply highlights how the dress of a person clearly defines who they are. In this case, these cheerleaders were wearing the uniforms they were given, and yet the obvious conclusion made was that because they were skimpy, these girls had no right to complain. Tell me, what does one thing have to do with the other? Is it because if you agree to wear skimpy clothes for your work, it automatically means you do not have a brain? It becomes quite clear that these biases are ingrained in our way of thinking, both by men and women.

However, in most instances, you do need to be as professional as your job requires, without going overboard.

Unfortunately, in some cases, you may very well lose this battle, depending on your work environment, as I demonstrated in the above example. Consider the opposite. If even wearing loose-fitting, baggy clothes, or attire such as scrubs, brings you unwelcome attention, perhaps the problem isn't what you are wearing or how you are wearing it but the simple fact that you are a woman and, as such, stir sexual thoughts in others. This is a situation you will have to evaluate carefully. Be honest with yourself in terms of the perceptions of women in general in your work place. It may be time to find a different job if you want to be taken seriously by your boss or your staff as a valuable contributor to your team.

Here's another recent example that highlights why dressing appropriately is important. Recently, I was shopping with my twenty-year-old daughter and we entered a store known for its high-quality, beautiful, trendy clothes. Let me clarify that this was not a lingerie store. As we entered, we noticed that the female store clerks were dressed in extremely provocative outfits. One in particular stood out: she was wearing mini-shorts with stiletto heels and an unbuttoned blouse completely revealing her bra underneath.

It's difficult to consider asking the opinion of a person who purposely dresses like this how something looks. In fact, I'm not sure I would value her opinion at all. Yet she was specifically employed to assist customers by helping to style them. She certainly had the opportunity to dress quite stylishly with the clothes this particular store sold—in other words, be attractive but not provocative. I understand that sex sells. Provocative ads constantly surround us. However, this is a mindset that needs to change if we are going to make any progress on the road to becoming empowered women and leaders in this world. We, as women, must start by addressing these insults to our personhood through our actions. As an example, we are visually assaulted by store windows displaying mannequins scantily clad in lingerie and yet have become immune to the message being sent. In fact, we seem to have allowed this to happen without much of a fight. Yes, sex sells, but at what cost to our overall self-esteem?

Aside from the clothes you wear, posture also can show how you feel about yourself. Are you portraying confidence, or are you shy, timid, or scared? Holding your shoulders square and set with your back straight and no evidence of slouching will help exhibit an air of confidence in whatever situation you walk into. Women, however, tend to slouch more frequently than men, perhaps hiding the fact they have breasts, perhaps trying not to be as tall as their male counterparts. Whatever the reason, we must stand up tall, be seen, and show we truly are a force to be reckoned with.

Think of our young heroine's example. Although at first she had to dress as a man to be noticed and listened to, after her true identity as a female was revealed, her manner of dress became that of a confident person—not sexy and not masculine, simply appropriate for her time.

The clothes you wear and the way you present yourself are important; speech is also a critical factor that demonstrates empowerment. The inflections in your voice and the power in your statements (without shouting) will impress even those around you who are used to Harvard-type lingo. The more distinct, articulate, and confident you are in what you say, the more respect you will earn from your colleagues.

When you are at work, hold your head high, keep your shoulders straight and square, and speak with excellent articulation and in a positive manner. The constant verbalization of "I believe," not "I think," will begin to pave the path of empowerment in any situation.

A woman should also be direct, looking eye to eye at whoever she is talking to. Never look down when talking to someone, or appear flustered. Never bat those eyelashes to be cute or innocent. Our facial expressions say as much or more than the clothes we wear or how we speak. Sometimes a steely look that portrays no nonsense will convey that exact message. Your discussions at work should never be polluted by the look of a wanderlust woman or portray any coyness in attitude. These will only be seen as areas of weakness, and respect will fly out the window, so to speak. You have opinions and thoughts that are as important as those of your male counterparts, so don't demean yourself by portraying weakness in expressing those thoughts or opinions. Remember to always see yourself as an important team member or even the leader in whatever discussions are occurring.

When you picture Condoleezza Rice, you see an extremely confident woman, both in dress and in posture. She imbues the characteristics often seen in confident men, but she isn't a masculinized version.

Exude confidence through your facial expressions, the way you stand and dress, and how you articulate your message. If you need to practice, stand in front of a mirror or have someone take a video while you practice. That way, you can more clearly see the areas you may need to change in order to demonstrate to others the confidence that really belongs to you.

This advice can work just as well at home, when interacting with your partner. Your facial expressions and posture are just as important in personal relationships. Clear articulation at home is critical to a successful relationship, especially in avoiding mind games. As women, we must move away from the damsel-in-distress role, regroup our inner confidence, and demonstrate equal partnership. We do not live in a soap opera and should never act as if we did. Decisions about how to raise the kids, personal finances, even the day-to-day simple things like what restaurant to go to for dinner, are the stage on which we empower ourselves in front of our partners and our children. Vengeful or mean-spirited speech will do nothing to bring those relationships toward respectful territory; it will only highlight to our children negative attributes that initially may bring us respect using fear, but will nonetheless backfire eventually.

Here's a great quote from an e-card:

> *Having a vagina doesn't stop me from believing that my balls are bigger than yours!*

I would amend it to the following:

> *Having boobs and a vagina doesn't stop me from asserting who I am, what I know, and what my expertise is. My balls may not be external, but they exist internally and I will use them to the best*

of my ability to get my point across and be listened to.

Confidence: The ability to show others—through dress, posture, and speech—that you have the experience and knowledge to make decisions concerning the task at hand, in a manner that demands respect but not fear.

WORKSHEET ON EXUDING CONFIDENCE

How do you see the attribute of CONFIDENCE in yourself demonstrated to others?

To allow CONFIDENCE to be visible to others, you must first feel it in yourself.

How can you help foster CONFIDENCE in yourself? Once you know CONFIDENCE is a part of who you are:

What challenges does your work environment have that inhibit your CONFIDENCE?

What challenges does your home environment have that inhibit your CONFIDENCE?

How can you strengthen your CONFIDENCE?
    At work
    At home

Goals to bring your CONFIDENCE to the forefront:
    At work
    At home

If you are unable to exhibit CONFIDENCE, what do you need to do to move forward to make it possible for others to see confidence in you?
    At work
    At home

How will having CONFIDENCE change your life?
    At work
    At home

Chapter Ten

Attribute #2: Work as Part of the Team but Maintain Your Visionary Goal

The Fairy Tale Version

Once upon a time, in a land far away and in the future, there lived a young princess. She belonged to a distant star galaxy and was a driven, dedicated woman with a forceful personality. This princess's story describes her as a fierce warrior who, like our first heroine, wanted to save her people. However, the major difference between the two was that this princess needed the help of others to accomplish her visionary goals.

Initially, she had difficulty with this particular attribute. I think secretly she would have preferred to do the job herself; however, she finally understood that she needed others to be successful in her endeavors. Unlike our first heroine, who relied on herself to fight and save her people, this princess had to work with others. Therefore, she demonstrated the attribute of working as part of a team to realize her success. This is an impressive attribute to teach and learn and is integral to being an empowered woman.

An alternate ending would have shown our young princess unwilling to accept help from others. In that case, she probably would not have successfully fought against the dark forces, and the galaxy would have been overtaken by evil. Knowledge would have been eliminated, and there would have been no chance for good to prevail. This would have been the outcome—all because she decided she could do it all.

Thankfully, that was not the ending. After all, once you lose to evil forces, getting back to the good around you becomes extremely difficult—both in fairy-tale land and in the real world.

The Modern Era Empowered Woman

Let's examine Golda Meir. She was the fourth elected prime minister of Israel. She came to the job knowing she had to deal with many factions of the Israeli government to maintain her goal of growing the young state of Israel. This meant she had to negotiate with all these factions and get them to work together as a team in order to accomplish her goals of keeping Israel safe and unified. She was the elected leader, remarkably, in an environment that frequently devalues women. She had to speak with and demonstrate leadership to Middle Eastern men whose opinions of women tended to be quite low—in some cases, equating a woman's value with that of livestock. Yet, she was able to be an effective, powerful, and revered leader of the fledgling state of Israel.

She could not do it alone. She knew she needed to rely on others to turn the newly dreamt-of nation into the reality it has become. She was criticized for some of her decisions; however, her decisions were never made in a vacuum. In fact, one of the heaviest criticisms lobbied at her came about because of the Yom Kippur War. However, the commission that was formed to investigate her said, "She decided wisely, with common sense and speedily, in favor of full mobilization of the reserves, as recommended by the chief-of-staff, despite weighty political considerations, thereby performing a most important service for the defense of the state."

Therefore, by working as part of a team, she was able to mitigate harsher criticism concerning her decisions, since these decisions were made together with others and not unilaterally. Because of her vision for Israel, she was able to bring all the parties to the table to ensure the success of this fledgling nation.

Golda Meir was a wise woman. She knew she needed to involve her entire cabinet in her decision-making so she could have buy-in from everyone. She accomplished that and so much more.

The Antithesis

A modern-day woman demonstrating the opposite of working as part of the team would make decisions on her own without regard to those around her. She would assume her decisions were correct, no matter who or what was destroyed along the way. Her motto would be that a leader knows best and needs no one to stand in her way.

My Experience

The following is a more day-to-day example: rounds at the hospital. When I do hospital rounds with my team, I'm the leader of that team. My visionary goal is that I provide the best care possible for each patient. However, that doesn't preclude me from being a part of the team as well and listening to everyone's input on a particular patient. Therefore, as a team, decisions are made about the care plans for that particular patient on that particular day. As the leader, I focus my team's discussions on the ultimate goal of getting that particular patient healthy and home.

I have seen the exact opposite happen with other teams. In those cases, when the discussions begin about care plans, those of the other members of the team are shot down and the physician in charge has the final say. Although the vision is there, the ability to incorporate the whole team to bring this goal to fruition is absent. A great deal of resentment builds with this approach, until team members feel like nothing more than scribes, writing down orders to be filled.

You may think the results obtained are the same either way. However, if, as a leader of the team, you ignore what others are suggesting, you run the risk of ultimately making a wrong decision and possibly causing harm rather than benefiting the situation—or, in the case of medical rounds, harming the patient.

Let's look at this a different way. If you think of a team not as a group of people but as the eyes, ears, and nose (sensory body) of an entity working for the good of a patient, you can see the fallibility of the leader (brain) making decisions in a void without the input of the rest of the team, i.e., the sensory body. Even though the brain is the entity that comes up with the goal, it can't accomplish it without the participation of all the sensory systems.

This same example applies to any team working for a company. This is how any successful corporation truly works: the team members are the sensory operators that provide information to the leader—the brain, so to speak, of the company. As an empowered woman, you want to be that leader, or, if you have not achieved that position yet, you want to be, at the very least, a valuable asset to that team. You want to be a member everyone respects and listens to.

A female colleague who has worked for many years at a hospital in another state related an example to me. Her encounter had to do with getting some of her colleagues within her group (all men) to understand the concept of a team working together. She had noticed, through the lack of referrals to her particular unit, that there was a misperception of what her team was capable of doing. The colleagues in her group believed, instead, that she dictated what needed to be done rather than allowing the team to help make decisions based on the best care possible for each patient.

Remember our previous discussions? Some men tend to believe that a woman who dictates is acting like a man and therefore is obviously out of her league; she needs to be put in her place. Some men also believe that a woman who behaves this way needs to be disciplined. In her case, the discipline came in the form of not getting any referrals, i.e., sending her patients elsewhere as well as being critical of the care provided by the team.

Sound familiar? In fact, since the majority who believed this were men, you can understand why. They were used to using their authoritative powers in their respective departments to make decisions. That is what is expected of men. According to them, it's the natural order of the universe. They may not have expertise in certain areas, but rather than referring a patient to a woman physician—especially one who is acting, in their opinion, like a man—they opt to keep a patient, whether it's what is best for that patient or not.

This particular style of management has been well documented in recent medical journal articles that describe the differences found between male and female physicians in terms of leadership traits. Men tend to dictate while women tend to work as a team. Since working as a part of a team is what women tend to do, they are therefore seen as less powerful or effective. The dominant role so often portrayed in male leadership is more highly valued and perceived to be more successful. It seems that if you have to ask others' opinions, it weakens you as a physician and leader. A woman should always ask opinions, but also always bend to what the man thinks it's best to do.

So, in order for my friend to rectify these faulty perceptions, it was necessary for her to send a letter to her colleagues. This letter was to remind them of how she and her team operate in her department and that, in fact, she was not, nor has she ever been, the person who "knows it all." Rather, she is the person with the vision for implementing cutting-edge therapies and who works together with her team's collective expertise. This is what truly allows an innovative approach in the treatment of patients to become a reality. This is the model that results in the successful outcomes she has continuously demonstrated.

She also confided to me that she really wanted to remind them in the letter that it's always about the patient, not their personal egos. But she knew that would have further inflamed the situation rather than allow her to be seen as extending a peace offering. After all, had she stated that in her letter, I'm sure she would have been labeled as aggressive—which, by these men's standards, again, is totally unacceptable for a woman.

The more incredulous part of this story is that prior to sending this letter, she was perceived as superior to others. What they failed to realize was that, as a leader, she was also a part of the team, a team that had expertise and excellence in diagnosis and treatment strategies in specific clinical scenarios. After she sent this letter, she did start to see a modest increase in referrals because of her public "confession" of not knowing everything and needing to rely on others for help.

To most of the men in her group, she satisfied the criteria of a woman who serves, as part of a group, rather than dictates what needs to be done. Although you might consider this a failure on her part to assert herself, she actually showed that, like our second princess, working together as part of a team while retaining the visionary goal as the leader resulted in success. She did clarify to me, however, that not everyone bought into the explanation in her letter. It was obvious to her and to me when she told me her story that the same "Good Ol' Boys Club" outliers will never change. They would rather remain stubborn and keep patients who should probably be transferred than accede to a woman whom they believe is acting like a bitch. Within her department, her ability to participate as a part of a team has afforded her a great deal of respect. Her team understands that although she continues to be the person with the vision for excellence in care, she still relies on them to make it a reality. In fact, her team at work was very supportive of the letter she sent out, hoping the results would speak for themselves.

In the end, her leadership qualities have, for the most part, won out, and patients have slightly more often been appropriately referred and taken care of. The lesson learned, however, is that we can't win all the battles despite our best intentions.

My hope is that little by little, through our perseverance in developing true leadership qualities, we will demonstrate to others our value as women leaders. Eventually, the old guard will no longer be the role models, and "The Good Ol' Boys Club" will become extinct. I can only hope this will happen sooner than later; it really does get old dealing with these dinosaurs.

My Advice

Exuding your personal confidence while at the same time respectfully listening to others will only boost your team's confidence and create an environment where everyone feels themselves to be an important part of the team. It will also generate respect for your ability to not only have a vision but, at the same time, value everyone's opinion and discuss openly the validity of those opinions. This isn't a sign of weakness but of tremendous strength.

Working as part of a team does not mean it compromises the person you are or what you believe in. In fact, you demonstrate leadership by listening to others, even if you aren't yet the leader. When you examine my friend's personal story, you might think she lowered herself to obtain the objective of getting more referrals. On the contrary, by pointing out that she wanted to pursue a vision but also needed the team's expertise to help her acquire her vision of taking care of complicated patients, she allowed others to see the bigger picture. To this day, she continues to be the leader of her team, but her success continues to come from everyone's input.

In the end, decisions that are made as a collaborative team, with everyone's input being valued and respected, create the foundations needed to build upon to achieve leadership roles. If you decide to adopt the masculine way of leading, you will not be accepted as a true leader but instead be thought of as a know-it-all bitch, just like my friend was—erroneously, of course. Again, it was not until she clarified that she had a whole team working in concert with her that she regained respect.

This advice becomes even more relevant when at home. Remember the old adage that marriage is hard work? I don't believe this is true—not if you work as a team, making decisions together after listening to each other respectfully. Having common goals is also very important. It's only considered compromise if one partner feels their thoughts or ideas weren't even taken into account.

I always tease my husband about a great line in the movie *My Big Fat Greek Wedding:* The man of the house is always the head, but the woman of the house is the neck—and it's the neck that turns the head in the direction it wants to go.

In reality, in a relationship that works well, no one person is the head or neck; instead, both are equal partners in the relationship. Blame can't be volleyed at one or another when you both work toward decisions together.

The problems begin when one person makes the decisions and those decisions create financial or personal problems. This is where you will see the breakdown of that relationship because the team no longer exists. Blame will be laid on the person who acted independently. If the results of the decision caused a successful outcome, resentment can develop in the person not involved with the decision, especially if the other person brags about his or her successful decision. Either way, there are no winners.

There is one caveat, both for work and for your personal relationship, in terms of using the team approach: sometimes, within that team, we have to agree to disagree. However, the leader in the work relationship needs to make the final decision. Within the personal relationship of partners, however, both parties are equal, and a compromise will need to be reached. As part of that partnership, we always hope these situations are few and far between.

Compromise should be, in any case, acceptable to both parties, and therefore the results should not create stress or resentment in any one person.

Teamwork: An effective team member maintains a visionary goal. This person is a respected team member working within a group for the greater good of that group and beyond. An empowered leader within the team is the person who has the vision and allows the team to make it a reality.

WORKSHEET ON BEING A TEAM PLAYER

How do you see the attribute of being a team player portrayed to others?

To allow the attribute of BEING A TEAM PLAYER to be visible to others, you must first feel it in yourself.

How can you help foster the attribute of BEING A TEAM PLAYER in yourself? Once you know BEING A TEAM PLAYER is a part of who you are:

What challenges does your work environment have that inhibit your ability to BE A TEAM PLAYER?

What challenges does your home environment have that inhibit your ability to BE A TEAM PLAYER?

How can you strengthen your ability to BE A TEAM PLAYER?
    At work
    At home

Goals to bring your ability to BE A TEAM PLAYER to the forefront:
    At work
    At home

If you are unable to exhibit the ability to BE A TEAM PLAYER, what do you need to do to move forward to make it possible for others to see this attribute in you?
    At work
    At home

How will BEING A TEAM PLAYER change your life?
    At work
    At home

Chapter Eleven

Attribute #3: Respect Others and Never Compromise

The Fairy Tale Version

Once upon a time there was a beautiful princess with hair as black as ebony, lips as red as cherries, and skin as white as snow. Unfortunately, she was the victim of her own beauty and was banished to the woods. There she met up with a group of dwarfs that helped her survive. Even though this princess had seen beauty her whole life, and the dwarfs were definitely not what one would describe as beautiful, she respected each of them and their quirks, including the grumpy one and the one who was dopey. To her, each one was a unique, valuable individual. She showed no prejudice because of their looks or idiosyncrasies. This trait of being respectful earned her the group's trust, which helped her survive and flourish. She was then able to escape her evil stepmother's plan to have her killed. In the process of trusting, this princess took command of the situation and was triumphant at the end.

The alternate ending would have read differently, of course. After escaping into the woods, the princess would have been mistrustful and disgusted by the dwarfs and would never have accepted their offer of protection. Eventually, she would have either starved in the forest or been captured by the huntsman and killed. The evil queen would have remained the fairest of them all, and that would have been the end of all beauty in the kingdom.

As in the real world, when we lose sight of what truly needs to be respected for its inherent value—not its superficial value—we lose the battle of reason, clarity, and, ultimately, compassion.

The Modern Era Empowered Woman

The late psychiatrist Elisabeth Kübler-Ross was well known for her description of the grieving process surrounding a loss. Yet her greater accomplishment, in my opinion, was identifying the need to respect those who are dying—as well as death itself.

Prior to her work, many people had a fear of terminally ill patients. It was not uncommon for those who were in the process of dying to be ignored and placed in a desolate area of the hospital or a private home until the inevitable happened. Thanks to her groundbreaking work, the concept of hospice arose. Around the world, hospice care has assisted terminal patients at the end of life, emphasizing respect in their care and comfort.

Kübler-Ross's leadership in understanding the concept of a dignified death is powerful. Without her groundbreaking work, end-of-life issues would still be relegated to the back burner, considered unimportant and a waste of time in terms of what it means to truly care for those patients with the respect due them. She believed that every person deserves a dignified death, surrounded by loved ones or caretakers who show respect, concern, and empathy.

The Antithesis

A modern-day woman demonstrating a lack of respect for others would act on her own, without regard for anyone's feelings or needs. She would never see the value in others, particularly those who were different from herself. She would be critical of others both at home and at work, and nothing would be good enough for her. Her demands would exceed the reality of what others would be capable of accomplishing. Her lack of respect would spill over into the differences in others' looks, physical abilities, and intellect. Even though everyone has something to offer that should be respected, she would never see value in these differences.

My Experience

Unfortunately, in the real world, I can honestly say this respectful nature is lacking in many workplaces today.

The personal stories I want to share concern difficult situations experienced by female colleagues as well as my own experiences. I have heard many stories from women in the workplace who were shown a complete lack of respect—both those who were leaders and those who were members of a team. Unfortunately, these experiences continue to highlight that, in terms of equal rights, women are still living in the Stone Age, waiting for the man to bring home the meat. It really is quite pitiful. The constant and unrelenting message is, "How could we ever be successful? We are only women."

I will tell you four stories that could probably be told in many forms to fit any workplace environment, whether it's a hospital, office, or other work setting. I'm sure you have stories of your own.

The first story revolves around the lack of respect shown to a female colleague for a concept of innovative care that she had brought to her hospital in another city. Her idea was to bring this innovative care to help treat patients who had suffered from a certain injury. This mode of therapy had already been successfully implemented in other major university hospital settings, and its success had been reported. She presented this therapy to her hospital committee to be considered and approved for implementation. The committee members listened to her plan and agreed with it, and she was able to implement this therapy at her hospital. So what's the problem, you ask?

Well, being part of a larger medical group that provides services to other hospitals in the city where she works, she ran into difficulties similar to those described in the previous chapter. Some members of her group (most of whom were male) were unsupportive of this new therapy and ignored the level of success she had achieved using it. (It's important to note that this success translated into positive patient outcomes as demonstrated by the database created to monitor outcomes.)

Interestingly, the non-medical community showed tremendous support for the new therapy, including giving positive media coverage about this cutting-edge technology. She had brought it to this particular hospital first, and it has remained the only hospital in the region offering this advanced therapy. However, within her group, little respect was afforded her for bringing it to the hospital and state. Instead, she was continuously questioned about her outcomes. She recently told me that the other members of her group still believe her outcomes aren't authentic, despite the data that continues to prove the contrary.

How can members of a group, i.e., the male members, act toward another member, a woman, in this fashion? I believe, in part, jealousy is the true culprit—jealousy because a woman showed them up. This is quite clear, since she also relayed that the women within her group have, for the most part, supported her as well as congratulated her on her success. After all, this success isn't hers alone; it translates to belonging to the whole group and, even more importantly, to the patient population being served.

She has since told me that the men in her group continue to be obstinate. She even overheard one of these same male colleagues say to others that she practices in the Dark Ages. He was so desperate to put her down that he continued to resort to unwarranted criticism. Unfortunately, for him, though, those that had heard his statements knew how off base he was, since her practice was anything but outdated—quite the contrary. He ended up apologizing to her for the statements he made by using the excuse that his comments were taken out of context—he was "just joking." Again, do you believe for a second he would have done this had it concerned another male colleague? I would have to answer that question with a resounding NO!

I have reminded her that their egos have clouded their judgment concerning innovative ideas that may make a difference in patients' lives. It seems that when respect is non-existent, jealousy may dominate. Where there is jealousy, lies and deception eventually may follow. In fact, this same woman physician experienced firsthand how lies are used when she was told to her face by another male colleague that she does not do as much work as she says she does during the day to support her team.

In this situation, he stated this in front of other women, among whom all but one did nothing to stop his lies and slanderous comments. In fact, when this other woman confronted him, he asked, "Are you calling me a liar?" To which this woman said, "Yes." Yet, nothing more was said by anyone else and the matter was dropped. I would venture to say that no one else spoke up because as women, they were afraid to voice their knowledge of the situation and risk being criticized.

Unfortunately, for my friend, this interaction has left a bitter taste in her mouth and, when she sees this particular physician, it takes everything in her being to be civil. It seems that, as long as men's perception of domination is preserved—along with their egos—they do not care if their actions result in less-than-adequate patient care, poor communication with others, or slanderous lies to be told.

My second story revolves around not being respected as a valuable member of a team. I happened to be on call one day, and we had a very difficult case because of the unusual presentation of this patient's illness. We had actually discussed, as a group, this patient on detailed rounds the day before and together had come up with a plan for this patient's care.

The next day, when I happened to be on call, the consultant (a male physician) involved in the case was not pleased with the care being given (even though it was the same care agreed upon by everyone, including himself, the day before). Rather than coming to me directly, since I was the person in charge of that patient that day, he called the medical director of the unit, at home, to complain. The medical director then called me to find out what was happening.

I was quite upset by the lack of respect I was being subjected to. Imagine how absurd it was that he felt more comfortable calling the male medical director at home rather than speaking directly with me—the person actually in the hospital, whom he had met and had had a previous discussion with. I called him on it immediately. I asked that he come to my office, which was near the patient ward. Although he was disrespectful to me in the way he handled his concerns, I was respectful to him by not arguing with him in front of others. I made it quite clear that he was never to go behind my back again. If he had concerns, he was to address them directly with me.

Because of his position within the hospital, he was quite taken aback that I confronted him. He finally apologized after trying to tell me the only reason he went to the other person first is because he had a well-established relationship with him.

Can I be frank? Bullshit! I can say that after our heated discussion, for a short time this type of interaction did not recur and he was cordial when we passed in the hallway. Unfortunately, despite being taken to task, he has again resorted to this type of inane behavior. Just prior to this book going to print, another similar incident occurred in which he did not communicate with me his decision concerning one of my patients, despite telling other staff members. Again, when confronted, he simply said we needed to set up a meeting to better establish forms of communication. Frankly, I believe the problem could be easily solved by simply texting me or picking up the phone and saying, "Hey, Cristina, I thought this patient should go to my unit after surgery because of this reason."

I'm continuously saddened by these altercations. They don't need to happen if respect for each other exists, regardless of your gender.

My third story also revolves around a particular patient's care and a difference of opinion on how to deliver said care. As the primary physician, I was orchestrating a patient's life support, which involved heart-lung bypass. This particular patient also required his body temperature to be lowered to help the brain maintain its integrity in the face of low oxygen delivery.

As the patient was placed on the heart-lung bypass machine, the surgeon involved—who, again, was merely a consultant—told the bedside nurses to remove the machine that allowed the patient's body temperature to be lowered. He felt that the heart-lung bypass machine could adequately deliver this therapy.

I immediately corrected him and stated that the other device was necessary and told him why. He was quite surprised I had contradicted him; it was something he wasn't used to hearing.

After he left, one of the surgical nurses in the room said, "Yes! Finally, someone was able to show him he didn't know everything." If this physician had shown respect for those around him, he wouldn't have barked orders without discussing the situation with those present, who were intimately involved with the care of this patient. This same physician just recently had an antagonistic argument with me at the bedside of a patient, in front of others, complete with eye-rolling and other body language that was viewed by others as uncalled for and demeaning to all members of the team. Some people never learn.

My final example continues to highlight the effects of a lack of respect for a woman colleague from one of her male colleagues. This particular woman physician had started treatment therapy on a patient who, she had determined, had qualified for the therapy. She signed out to the physician on call and left for the evening. When she returned the next morning to take over care for the day, she found that this physician had taken her patient off the treatment, simply stating, "Your patient did not really qualify for using this, so I stopped it before it was completed." Not surprisingly, this patient went on to develop complications that might have been avoided had the therapy been continued as originally planned.

The woman physician's response to her male counterpart was astonishment at his action. He continued to chastise her for her poor judgment. There were no apologies and no review of the case so that this male physician could learn to improve his practice to benefit his patients. His lack of respect for her as a colleague, together with denying that this woman knew what she was talking about (in fact, she did know more than he did in this particular case) was so great that he could not get beyond his own ego to listen and be respectful of her medical opinion. In essence, his care of this patient was also less than adequate, all because he refused to listen to a woman. In his eyes, how could a woman know more than him? What blasphemy!

Unfortunately, this particular male physician is an older gentleman who is originally from a country that consistently devalues women. My guess is that he will never change how he perceives the role of women in today's society. If his attitude only affected individual women in routine, mundane decisions, perhaps it could be overlooked as coming from the old guard that will eventually disappear. However, this person has patients under his care who are directly affected by the decisions he makes. It isn't okay for him to continue to practice like this. Even more unfortunate is that the group this physician belongs to has done nothing to reprimand his behavior. There is no accountability for his poor medical care. Certainly, worse than this, justice was not served for this patient. We know that the adverse outcome was directly related to the male physician's decision not to follow the female physician's recommendations.

But, in today's culture, where suing for slander is commonplace, it becomes difficult to address these issues even when they are taken higher up the chain to medical committees that address these types of issues. More often than not, situations like these are swept under the rug with the excuse of, "He'll be retiring soon." In this particular situation, I'm sure the male physician could have found an expert witness to disagree with my friend's assessment of the need for this particular treatment plan. Medicine, after all, is sometimes as much an art as it is a science. Although my colleague was devastated, she will continue to practice medicine to the best of her abilities. The sad fact remains that her patient will be affected for the rest of his life because of the less-than-adequate care he received—all because a woman's care plan was questioned by a male colleague.

This form of inequity will be difficult to stop unless one of two things happens: either patients become aware of the dilemma and demand better care or sue, or insurance companies trend consistently poorer outcomes to certain individual physicians and remove them from their plans. Until the culture truly changes, this is how these situations will need to be addressed.

My Advice

What I want to emphasize is to never compromise your goals, your ideals, or your vision because you are a woman. In any situation, you must first and foremost always respectfully listen to and discuss other people's ideas. However, if they do not mesh with your goals, you should explain why they wouldn't work and move on. Look that person square in the eyes, explain to them that just because you are a woman doesn't mean you don't have "balls," and therefore they should respect you as they respect other colleagues who anatomically have them. Regrettably, in this last case I mentioned, there was nothing the woman physician could do to reverse what the male physician had done. That particular therapy had specific time constraints that could not be changed.

Again, in some situations, your only response is to continue to do your best and acquire support from others so that this type of behavior is severely discouraged. In the end, however, you and you alone must be able to stand in front of a mirror and respect the image looking back. Never forget that. If that means you believe the lack of respect shown to you has significantly affected others—whether other patients or other colleagues—you may need to bring your concerns to an authoritative figure that may be able to do something more drastic. Be prepared to present your case clearly, unemotionally, and with clarity. Present the results or effects of those decisions. As it's been said, "Truth will set you free."

And never forget that when all else fails, karma is a bitch. Eventually, the greater community will respect your decisions, and others will be better because of this.

As for the home front, it's similar to what we discussed in the previous chapter. A relationship is much like a work partnership. You should never feel you are compromising your ideals. You respect each other's opinions but come to an agreement that is satisfactory for each person. That is what makes any partnership work. Anything less is a perfect breeding ground for regret, resentment, and name-calling.

Lack of respect also can be seen in more heart-wrenching situations such as verbal or physical abuse. There is also the more subtle emotional abuse. These situations exist because one partner doesn't respect the other but instead feels he or she can have total control over that person. In circumstances where these actions are caused or accentuated by alcohol or drugs, you have not only the loss of respect but also a volatile situation where the person perpetrating the violent acts can lose all control.

These situations aren't remediable; you can't change that person, nor are they doing those things to you because it's your fault. That explanation is the worst type of self-deprecation. If you have reached that point, you need to immediately exit the relationship. There is no other solution. To stay could endanger your life and the lives of others in the household. Again, these behaviors aren't your fault; they belong to a person who doesn't have any self-respect and therefore can't give respect to others. That person will cover up this lack of self-respect by attempting to overpower you through words or physical actions. Do not be fooled—exit immediately.

Certainly, in less drastic situations in a relationship, if there is no respect in that marriage or partnership, why does that relationship even exist? Perhaps you feel that the other person will change or that you don't deserve better for whatever reason. In both cases, you are wrong. You have a choice. Cut your losses and find happiness in life with a true partner. Life is too short to feel degraded or to feel that whatever is happening in the relationship is your fault.

I know that all of this advice can be difficult to act upon. Many external factors or internal relationships are involved or will be impacted when drastic action is taken. However, in the long run, respect is everything. If you aren't being shown respect within a relationship, it will impact how others perceive you in the family unit. Remember, you are the role model that your children look up to. If you portray someone who doesn't deserve respect, you will be demonstrating that respect may not be attainable at all.

Respect: Respect is when others listen to your point of view, your ideas, and your thoughts, and consider them for what they are truly worth—and vice versa. Respect also involves understanding a situation for what it is and not judging it with preconceived notions. You must also have the capacity to be respectful to those around you. Remember, respect begets respect, and respect clearly segues into our next attribute—compassion and empathy.

WORKSHEET ON RESPECTING OTHERS

How do you see the attribute of RESPECTING OTHERS in yourself being demonstrated to others?

To allow RESPECTING OTHERS to be visible to others, you must first feel it in yourself.

How can you help foster RESPECT FOR OTHERS in yourself? Once you know RESPECT FOR OTHERS is a part of who you are:

What challenges does your work environment have that inhibit your ability to RESPECT OTHERS?

What challenges does your home environment have that inhibit your ability to RESPECT OTHERS?

How can you strengthen your ability to RESPECT OTHERS?
    At work
    At home

Goals to bring your ability to RESPECT OTHERS to the forefront:
    At work
    At home

If you are unable to exhibit the ability to RESPECT OTHERS, what do you need to do to move forward to make it possible for others to see this attribute in you?
    At work
    At home

How will having RESPECT FOR OTHERS change your life?
    At work
    At home

Chapter Twelve

Attribute #4: Be Compassionate and Show Empathy

The Fairy Tale Version

Once upon a time there was a young woman who was an accomplished reader. She also had many other traits, including being intelligent, independent, and a non-conformist. Yet one of her most wonderful qualities was compassion. She was able to feel compassion for a beast that terrified people in her village, mostly because of its looks. She was able to see past its "beastliness," which enabled her to show empathy. In fact, because of her compassion, she was able to break the spell this beast was under, and, consequently, the beast turned into a handsome prince.

Remember, however, that the prince had been placed under this spell because he had lacked compassion for others. Therefore, the young woman's actions teach us two things: first, without compassion, the world would continue to judge on looks alone and be a frightening place to live. Second, the compassion she showed for another allowed that person to also become more compassionate toward others, thereby releasing him from his miserable beastly spell.

The alternate and less desirable ending would have been for this young lady to be disgusted by the ugly beast and allow the villagers to kill him. The beast never would have been released from his spell and therefore never would have understood the meaning of true love. The girl in the story would have married only for looks and status, and she probably would have lived an unhappy life.

In the real world, showing indifference to those around us who are suffering (whether physically or emotionally) can wreak havoc on society as a whole. Each person who propagates this indifference allows the next person to continue this model solely for the convenience of not getting involved. After all, it's easier to ignore a distasteful situation than to get involved and make an effort to help.

We will see, in the modern woman's example and in my personal experiences, what each behavior reaps in terms of individuals and society as a whole.

The Modern Era Empowered Woman

If we look to a modern-day woman to demonstrate the attribute of compassion, I believe that Florence Nightingale fits the bill perfectly.

Florence Nightingale (1820–1910) is known as the founder of modern nursing. However, this title came about because of the compassion she showed in caring for troops during the Crimean War. At that time, medicines were in short supply and hygiene was neglected. As a result, infections were prevalent, many of which were fatal.

An excerpt from *The Times* describes her as, "A ministering angel without any exaggeration in these hospitals… every poor fellow's face softens with gratitude at the sight of her. When all the medical officers have retired for the night… she may be observed alone, with a little lamp in her hand, making her solitary rounds."

That type of compassion—any type of compassion—translates to someone who cares enough to go out of her way to make a difference, which is, in essence, what empathy is. Remember, lip service doesn't count.

Compassion can take many forms. One form of compassion is in the understanding of another person's viewpoint, whether there is agreement or not. This form of compassion involves respect, as we have talked about previously, and it allows every person to show they have value both as a person and as a co-worker. Compassion also is shown when we take care of those less fortunate than we are, whether economically or health-wise. This action also demonstrates empathy.

As a team member, you need to demonstrate both compassion and empathy. One doesn't seem to exist without the other. You can see how all of these concepts are tied together; one can't operate without the other.

The Antithesis

When observing modern-day women, you will find, from time to time, that some do not seem to understand the concept of compassion or empathy because they also lack the ability to be respectful toward others. They will act according to what best serves their own interests. Unfortunately, the best way to treat these women at work, as difficult as it may be, is to remain firm in your beliefs. Make the best of the situation and continue to do the work you believe is right.

At home, these women will speak to their partners or children with disrespect and, at times, disdain. They believe this form of communication is effective in bringing the results they want in their personal lives. In their minds, compassion is seen as a form of weakness—being a pushover. Nothing could be further from the truth.

My Experience

A lack of compassion (using a general example) might be displayed in a physician performing a quick office visit rather than a longer, more comprehensive exam. It also might mean that the physician could bill more each day because that person sees more patients. Doing this, in the long run, could compromise the patients' lives.

Another example might be that of a hospital administrator who places best patient healthcare practices secondary in importance to the financial bottom line. This, of course can adversely affect patient care. Examples are seen across the country.

For instance, it's well recognized in today's business practices that, because of insurance issues, hospital administrators may be more apt to retain patients to increase the hospital's revenue. Therefore, the treatment services provided for certain illness might actually be sub-optimal to upgraded services found at other hospitals that are considered by industry standards to be centers of excellence. In other words, not all hospitals are created equal. There are some hospitals that have greater expertise in treatment of certain illnesses. Therefore, although the care provided at each hospital is basic and equal, there are some hospitals that are better equipped for certain patients' needs. Unfortunately, patients don't know there may be better places with better success rates where they can be treated, and, therefore, they don't know to ask to be sent or transferred. They trust their physician to tell them what is best for them.

However, in today's hostile financial environment, doctors are many times forced to keep these patients at the less-optimal hospitals because they know that hospital administrators will reprimand them—or worse, replace them—if they transfer patients too often. I actually know of a group of physicians that a hospital replaced with another group because the first group was sending too many patients elsewhere. Therefore, we, as physicians, are now faced with losing privileges for doing the right thing.

Eventually, insurance companies will become wiser when they start seeing firsthand the unnecessary increased length of stay or less than optimal outcomes of patients because they aren't receiving the appropriate treatment in a timely fashion. Of course, poorer outcomes translate to greater overall costs of care over the lifetime of a patient. Until they see this, however, these situations will continue to occur. In the future, when the above becomes obvious, correct decisions will be made—but not for the reasons we would hope would guide them.

I digress, however. My point is simply that without compassion, incorrect decisions will be made. It doesn't matter what scenario is represented, medical or non-medical. Outside the world of medicine, large corporations also can lose their compassion for the individual or the masses. Their lack of compassion may induce them to produce inferior products just to cut costs. This decision can then result in the loss of good professionals and the loss of quality products, along with the possibility of compromising safety because the bottom line becomes the priority.

A recent example was the horrific fire in Bangladesh at a clothes factory supplying American retailers. Over one thousand people lost their lives in that fire, which stemmed from poor working conditions and an unsafe environment. These less-than-adequate working conditions existed because they allowed the manufacturer to produce clothing at a drastically low cost to sell to American retailers. The factory's competitors manufactured clothing at a higher cost, either in the U.S. or elsewhere, in facilities that were safer and more appropriate. This cost discrepancy provided the incentive for companies to accept the potential risks of producing lower-cost products.

The American public needs to be aware of the decisions being made by these corporations. Americans need to step up to the plate and not accept those risks just so they can purchase a lower-cost item. The lives of others are adversely affected daily so the consumer can buy a piece of clothing for a few dollars less than what the competitors offer.

I believe that this lack of compassion, seen across all areas of commerce or healthcare, really translates to a lack of ethics. Although the words "compassion" and "ethics" aren't synonymous, there is a quality they share that ultimately dictates that the right decision is made.

In the world of agriculture and animal-farming practices, we see many examples that show how the industrial revolution also propagated this lack of compassion, and, eventually, a lack of business ethics. Again, we see firsthand decisions being made only to propagate higher profits. In the end, the consumer is eventually adversely affected in areas of health. These links are finally being reported. Although the following example is more generic and not directly related to women's issues, I feel it clearly demonstrates the point I'm trying to make.

Let's take as an example the obscene choices our industrialized farms have implemented in order to produce fatter livestock— e.g., cows and chickens. These bad choices include feeding the animals rendered products from their own species, essentially making herbivores into carnivores and changing the pH of their stomach contents. This practice, in turn, allows harmful bacteria to propagate.

To counteract this problem, farmers use steroids, chemicals, and antibiotics, which then cause excessive weight and also allow antibiotic-resistant organisms to propagate. These animals develop crippling deformities and thus can experience great pain until the time of slaughter. The slaughter process itself is wrought with shortcuts, causing undue pain to the animals and potential contamination of the meat being processed. In fact, all the outbreaks we see in the news concerning the contamination of meat with *E. coli* come from cows, which, as they are being slaughtered, stool on themselves out of fear and pain. The meat then is ground up and contains these deadly bacteria, which are now showing up as resistant to commonly used antibiotics and therefore are more difficult to kill.

The process of slaughtering should allow the meat to be cleaned prior to this process; however, the slaughterhouse line goes so fast that some cows are still alive as they are being processed. The faster they can process the meat, the more profits are created per minute. Imagine, cows being skinned while still alive, baby chicks being thrown into grinders still alive, and pigs, one of the most intelligent of the domestic farm animals, also being processed while still alive. All this has been done and continues to be done so that the food industry can sell at greater profits. These aren't humane farms; they are farm factories whose goal is to turn a maximum profit. There is no place for humane treatment at these facilities. Such sentiments would slow down the assembly line and therefore decrease or obliterate the profits.

Sadly, we are witnessing another example of what happens when the bottom line becomes more important than the quality and safety of that product, let alone the ethical component that is obviously non-existent. As we all know, the consumer becomes the ultimate victim. Significant health issues develop not only secondary to unnecessary contamination of poorly processed meat but also because increased consumption has been linked to increased rates of cancer and heart disease.

After all, we are what we eat; if we eat meat from animals whose last minutes of life were wrought with pain and fear, what do you think was circulating through their bodies and muscle tissue as they were dying? Those stress-filled hormones they produced then make it into our bodies and continue to contaminate us in ways we are just now discovering.

The environment also suffers secondary to increased methane gases, which propagate global warming. The first victim is, of course, the farm animal that lived a miserable life and died a miserable death—all for the sake of making a higher profit.

At home, I would hope that a lack of compassion from your partner isn't even an issue. Who else can you turn to other than your life partner when the world seems a difficult place in which to live? Without that compassionate component in place, the relationship lacks the ability to grow in a positive manner with each experience.

Much like the example of the industrialization of farms, partners who stay in a relationship only for sake of convenience can affect a relationship, usually in a negative manner.

Let's consider the example of a fictitious couple that has been together for many years. Believe me, this isn't such a far-fetched example as you might initially think. For the sake of argument, let's say they have remained together only because of the convenience of what they continue to do for each other. You could surmise that this is a relationship solely built on maintaining the status quo, not on love or respect. If you were to witness how they speak to each other, you would hear in their voices a certain level of disdain. The lack of compassion would allow lies and deceit to enter and even go so far as to possibly affect their personal finances or their intimate life together.

The unfortunate part would be that, because this had been going on for a prolonged period of time, neither person could see what is happening and how far their relationship had deteriorated. If you were to ask either of them if they still loved each other, they would be adamant that they did. They would be in complete denial so that the status quo could be maintained. Yet anyone seeing their interactions would beg to differ.

Their initial lack of compassion for each other allowed indifference to creep in, replacing what probably was once a truly caring relationship built on respect and love. I'm sure this example isn't so foreign to you; perhaps you have seen certain degrees of the above example in people you know and their relationships—perhaps even in your own. If we look closely at situations like this, we will see the same pattern of progression of a deteriorating relationship, from a form of early love to convenience, to disdain, deceit, and finally indifference. The result of this equation is a lack of love and eventually loneliness within that relationship.

To prevent this from happening, compassion must re-enter the relationship. Compassion will beget respect and afford the possibility of salvaging the relationship. Without this critical component, consider the relationship doomed.

My Advice

Compassion comes in many forms. It comes in being a good listener. It comes in offers of help to an individual. It comes in the form of acknowledging that person as a valuable member of your team, of the human race, or of your relationship. Remember that each person is someone's son or daughter, someone who is loved or was once loved by others. They deserve, at the very least, your respectful attention.

Compassion as a society comes from collectively making the right, ethical decisions in regard to the products we purchase. Being an empowered consumer means you are aware of the process that got that food or item into your hands. It means you are willing to accept the cost of that item and feel that the appropriate decisions were made by the manufacturing company so that its production has not caused another's misery because of corporate greed.

Compassion is difficult to cultivate unless there is a seed or spark of that particular human quality inside you already. Even if that spark exists, it needs to be nurtured so it can encompass all aspects of your life, both at home and at work. It can only be nurtured by the understanding and continual practice of knowing there are others more important than you. It also comes from the knowledge that the universe doesn't revolve solely around you. That isn't to say that you are less important than others, only that you must always keep others in mind and act ethically according to everyone's best interests.

However, in the situation where you find no compassion in your relationship, a change should occur so that compassion re-enters your life. Sometimes, simply talking with your partner is all that is needed to raise awareness. However, if your partner truly lacks compassion, you must not lose your attribute of compassion. Leave that relationship and seek compassion elsewhere. If you lose yours, you will lose a vital part of yourself that would otherwise help complete you as an empowered woman. No situation or relationship is worth this loss.

Compassion: A trait that allows a person or corporation to act ethically by thinking of others above themselves and not judging others by looks, status, or the situation in which they find others.

Compassion is tightly intertwined with respect.

WORKSHEET ON BEING COMPASSIONATE AND SHOWING EMPATHY

How do you see the attribute of COMPASSION in yourself demonstrated to others?

To allow COMPASSION to be visible to others, you must first feel it in yourself.

How can you help foster COMPASSION in yourself? Once you know COMPASSION is a part of who you are:

What challenges does your work environment have that inhibit your COMPASSION?

What challenges does your home environment have that inhibit your COMPASSION?

How can you strengthen your COMPASSION?
    At work
    At home

Goals to bring your COMPASSION to the forefront:
    At work
    At home

If you are unable to exhibit COMPASSION, what do you need to do to move forward to make it possible for others to see compassion in you?
    At work
    At home

How will having COMPASSION change your life?
    At work
    At home

Chapter Thirteen

Attribute #5: Be Humble and Know You Are Constantly Learning

The Fairy Tale Version

Once upon a time there lived a young woman whose family made her feel subservient to them. They even made her an outcast and treated her as a servant. Yet throughout her trials, she remained humble and never looked down on others, even when she acquired the status of a princess.

Her lesson is a powerful one. It brings hope that every person will see value in others. Humility goes beyond respect because it challenges a person to look within and find the imperfections that make us all human. In fact, true humility is rarely found in others, although unfortunately the opposite—arrogance—is very prevalent.

Is it possible to be humble and still exude confidence and compassion and be an important member of a team, or a leader who is respected? Certainly you see it in this fairy tale.

In the alternate, darker version, this particular girl would exact a painful vengeance on those who put her in a subservient position and treated her with cruelty. By behaving this way, she would be no better than the characters that treated her unfairly from the beginning.

In the real world, we will see that being humble is different from respecting others. The trait of humility allows a person to know that he or she is no better or more important than the next person, and that everyone has value to society as a whole. The lack of humility that we see in the world today creates a society where everyone feels they are better than the next person and is constantly trying to prove it. In a world of humble people, the discussion of who is best would then become less important than the ideal of working together to create a better world for all.

The Modern Era Empowered Woman

What better role model in real life can one find for the attribute of humility than Mother Teresa? She embodied humility in her words and especially in her actions. She founded the Missionaries of Charity, which continue to run hospices and homes for people with AIDS/HIV, leprosy, and tuberculosis. This group also operates soup kitchens, children and family counseling programs, orphanages, and schools around the world. The motto of this organization is to give "wholehearted and free service to the poorest of the poor."

Humility comes in many forms. In real, everyday life, the type of humility Mother Teresa displayed may be difficult to find, because servitude to the poor is seen by many as inconvenient.

In terms of the work environment, humility can take on another form. Let me explain further.

When you find a person who is humble at work, you will find a person who knows what their limits are in terms of their knowledge as well as abilities. This is a person who will ask many questions to better understand the situation at hand.

The Antithesis

A modern-day woman who demonstrates the opposite of humility is one who appears to know everything—or she is autocratic, so it's her way or the highway. The opposite of humility can also be described as arrogance. When a person believes they know everything there is to know, or that they have all the knowledge needed, or that they are the best in their field, watch out—disaster will strike that person and possibly the workplace.

At home, being arrogant or autocratic also can lead to an unhappy personal life, where the other partner feels totally devalued and is reduced to feelings of uselessness.

Cultivating humility will go a long way in helping you reach your goals and showing others you are truly a leader. There is a great quote I was once told: "The biggest obstacle to wisdom is the illusion of knowledge." (Anonymous)

Perhaps this quote is best illustrated in the following story.

My Experience

One day, about twenty years ago, a general surgeon needed to operate to remove a blood vessel in the chest cavity of a patient due to the blood vessel's aberrant flow to the lungs, which increased fluid in the lungs. When he opened the patient's chest, he found that the blood vessel had grown to the size of the major artery that delivers oxygenated blood to the rest of the body. In his haste and arrogance, he did not stop to consider that he might need the services of a cardiovascular surgeon to assist him. Instead, he proceeded to tie off what he believed to be the overgrown vessel. Probably you can imagine where this story is going—he tied off the major artery instead and caused an immediate code arrest in the patient. Again, instead of calling for help, he tried to undo the damage by re-attaching the major artery, but to no avail. The damage was irreversible, and the patient died on the table.

I know this sounds extreme, but it happened. It happened to a board-certified surgeon, a male surgeon, who felt he knew it all and needed no one else's help.

I now take you to a more recent example in which a similar situation involving a female surgeon occurred. When she opened the chest of her patient, she was surprised at the size of a vessel she thought was to be clipped. Instead of proceeding and possibly causing a tragic accident, she called for ultrasound assistance and was able to take out the correct aberrant vessel. The patient lived and had a complete recovery.

Again, both of these cases emphasize that humility doesn't mean you are stupid or lack knowledge. It means that you have the understanding that we all have a lot to learn from others and that occasionally we all need assistance from others. Eventually, understanding this concept will go a long way in enhancing your ability to benefit others. This will ultimately serve you in your quest to do the best job possible.

My Advice

Humility at work means having the ability to know your limits, ask for help, and feel empowered by knowing the outcome was optimized by your cautious, well-thought-out, non-arrogant actions.

At work, however, you might find yourself in a situation where one of your colleagues demonstrates a less-than-humble attitude. Perhaps providing this colleague with a gentle reminder that there are different ways to think through a problem and possibly come up with alternate solutions might be helpful.

Certainly, there are times when a person will be an expert in a situation that arises. It's always important to listen to that person, but never hesitate to ask questions. An idea may be triggered from such a question that might even surprise the expert. However, if this person refuses to entertain questions, then beware: you are looking at someone who may be less an expert and more an arrogant SOB. In these situations, remove yourself from any further discussions. Any attempts made to continue discussing the situation may eventually end badly, for you as well as whatever the situation might be.

Here's where it gets tricky when talking about the home front. Let's be clear about a very important fact: being humble at home doesn't mean being submissive to your partner—not financially, not with chores, and certainly not sexually. A bestselling novel that exploits the submissive nature of the female partner and portrays her as enjoying playing this part is a case in point. Let me repeat: there is no room in a relationship for one partner to be submissive to the other, not under any circumstances. Submission breeds disrespect for that person and allows the dominant person to feel superior to the other. Furthermore, I can't believe the argument that perhaps the submissive partner chose this path. The human spirit, at its core, can't willingly choose to accept a submissive role in any area of life. It goes against the instinct of survival, which is described as fight or flight. Submission has been artificially created to deal with power imposed by others. Period, end of story.

Being humble at home also implies that arrogance has no place there in dealing with your partner in day-to-day events as well as life goals. Being humble means asking questions, being respectful of each other's opinions and feelings, and coming out in a united front to the world. There is no room for the role of being submissive, nor are the words "submissive" and "humble" interchangeable. Never forget this. If you do, and this becomes the norm at home, don't expect to garner any respect. On the contrary, you will be used and abused, and you will suffer greatly in the self-esteem department. This will spill over into the rest of your life, including your work, which will eventually compromise your chances of showing leadership qualities.

When is enough, enough? When would pleasing your partner ever become more important than your self-respect and self-esteem? The answer is never. Any partner worth their salt would never allow your self-esteem to be trampled on for their own pleasure.

Remember, as I stated before, you must be able to look at yourself in the mirror and respect the person looking back at you. Enjoyment is a two-way street. The primal act of sex can certainly lend itself to roles of dominant and submissive, but it doesn't have to be that way anymore. We have rights as equal human beings, not only for receiving pleasure but also for giving pleasure. Neither of these instances requires one person to be submissive to the other.

It's important that, as mothers, we teach our daughters this very important lesson. They must never feel they have to give everything up to please another person. They must never feel that being demeaned as a person could result in anything but feeling ashamed, with the subsequent development of low self-esteem. Again, what they learn in their personal lives will spill over into their work. If all they know is being subservient to others, they will show low self-esteem and be submissive at work. No one will respect their thoughts or ideas. This becomes a cycle of misery between work and home, and their own children will suffer the consequences of having a poor role model.

Again, nothing good will come of perpetuating this lifestyle. Your home life as well as your life at work certainly will suffer.

Humility: Humility is the opposite of arrogance. It's the understanding that you aren't all-important, the ability to know your limits, to ask for help, and to feel empowered by knowing the outcome was optimized by your cautious, well-thought-out, non-arrogant actions.

Here is another great quote:

> *Being humble means that we aren't put on earth to see how important we will become, but to see how much difference we can make in the life of others.*
>
> Gordon B. Hinckley

This quote embodies the humility Mother Teresa showed as well as the humility found in the female surgeon who asked the right questions and sought help from others to ensure the well-being of her patient.

WORKSHEET ON HUMILITY

How do you see the attribute of HUMILITY in yourself demonstrated to others?

To allow HUMILITY to be visible to others, you must first feel it in yourself.

> How can you help foster HUMILITY in yourself?

Once you know HUMILITY is a part of who you are:

> What challenges in your work environment inhibit your HUMILITY?
>
> What challenges in your home environment inhibit your HUMILITY?

How can you strengthen your HUMILITY?
  At work
  At home

Goals to bring your HUMILITY to the forefront:
  At work
  At home

If you are unable to exhibit HUMILITY, what do you need to do to move forward to make it possible for others to see humility in you?
  At work
  At home

How will having HUMILITY change your life?
  At work
  At home

Chapter Fourteen

Attribute #6: Stay Calm During Times of Stress

The Fairy Tale Version

Once upon a time, in a land over the rainbow, a young girl traveled on a colorful brick road to find her way back home. Despite being in a strange land, with strange customs and creatures, she remained calm throughout her journey until she reached the solution that would take her home again. In the story, she never faltered, and she met each challenge with calm resolve, not panic. She reached her goal by trusting others, staying calm, and thinking through her problems.

Can you imagine the chaos that would have reigned if the alternate version were told? This girl would have been hysterical at each turn of the road and would have been unable to face her fears with thoughtfulness and calm resolve. She never would have been able to return to her own home, as she would have been too paralyzed by fear or uncertainty to act or to move forward in her quest.

In real life, becoming hysterical during times of stress only creates further hysteria in those around you. The following personal examples will better show you the consequences of such actions. No one can benefit from being unable to handle stressful situations. Instead, you must first weigh all your options, think about possible solutions, and choose the best road to take.

The Modern Era Empowered Woman

In a more recent example, we meet Rosa Parks, a civil rights champion, who remained calm during one of the most divisive and stressful times our country as gone through.

Her act of defiance was not by a show of force but by quietly remaining seated on a bus and refusing to give up her seat to a white person. In her autobiography, *My Story*, Ms. Parks said, "People always say that I didn't give up my seat because I was tired, but that isn't true. I was not physically tired... I was not old... No, the only tired I was, was tired of giving in."

In today's world, our lives are very stressful. Staying calm is always a challenge. The best way to show leadership at all times is to prioritize what needs to get done. Stress can escalate to a crisis situation; staying calm is of utmost importance.

You have all heard of nerves of steel, right? Well, those nerves of steel come with a clear mind that can think through times of great adversity.

The Antithesis

Not staying calm breeds hysteria, a trait from which, as women, we definitely need to distance ourselves. Hysteria results in poor judgments being made, with increased overall stress and less desirable outcomes at work. At home, hysteria or increased stress over situations can result in burnout within the relationship, where the partner stops listening and a "cry wolf" scenario is assumed.

My Experience

In my world, I have seen a cardiovascular surgeon holding a living, beating heart in his hands, close his eyes for a few seconds, and take a few deep breaths before proceeding onward.

Unfortunately, I have also seen the complete opposite—where a surgeon becomes so frustrated with the events unfolding before him in the operating theater that he starts throwing surgical instruments at the nurses, all the while screaming that he isn't in the company of qualified people. Such a surgeon is neither a great team player nor a confidence builder.

Which surgeon would you prefer to work with, and which do you believe is a true leader? Which is the empowered person?

Whether you are praying to a Higher Source or simply composing your nerves, take a few moments during times of stress to regroup. Your team feeds off your emotions. Calmness will breed calmness, while panic ripples through a crowd and escalates the fear component tenfold.

I have myself stood by many a patient who was dying despite our heroics to save their lives. In those situations, many of which were code resuscitations, you can clearly see why the utmost calmness must prevail. This calmness definitely demonstrates leadership qualities and helps the team involved to stay cohesive and work together to save that person's life.

Staying calm during a volatile situation can also de-escalate a potentially deadly situation. The case that comes to mind is a woman who was abducted by a person who was clearly in a state of mental anguish. She started to calmly read a book to him about how his life could have purpose. She was able to calm her abductor down to the point where he released her and sought help for himself. Of course, this is an extreme situation, and not all such crises will end like this, but this case demonstrates the power of staying calm during troubled times.

My Advice

Never mistake calmness for not caring about a situation. Although both emotions can appear the same, the act of not caring or lacking compassion about the situation also can affect the outcome—only in a negative fashion, as was described in the previous chapter. It is, of course, counterproductive to the qualities of empowerment we want to encourage.

I also want to clarify that the act of being calm should never take away that gut feeling you might have in any given situation involving stress. These feelings can guide your thoughts as to the best approach to the problem and thus bring calmness into the situation when it is so desperately needed.

Stress at home is a common denominator in most families. Imagine two people living together day after day, night after night. Then add the stresses of health issues, children, finances, and the outside world, in general. Unfortunately, stress at home is just as counterproductive to achieving a plan of action for whatever problem is at hand.

Again, being calm doesn't indicate you don't care about a situation, and it doesn't mean you aren't going with your gut feeling about the problem, either.

Here's where taking a few moments to re-group, whether in your car before entering the house or in the middle of a heated discussion, can benefit the partnership. We all know that during stressful times, things often are said in the heat of the moment that would have been better left unsaid. Perhaps they were hurtful or were just plain mean. We can prevent this with a moment of silence. Just as we tell our kids to count to ten, we should do the same. It really works.

Working through health issues or financial problems can be even more challenging. Remember, however, that shouting, screaming, or walking out on the other person does nothing to begin to find solutions to the problem at hand. Instead, these maneuvers simply create a block in communications, which then further hampers any efforts to calmly troubleshoot solutions that might be helpful.

I understand that this is easier said than done; however, I never said that staying calm would be easy. It's counterintuitive to the fight or flight response that is programmed into all living things.

Clearly, in the most dire of situations, there may be no solutions. This is when remaining calm becomes extremely challenging. However, it's in those dire situations when we see this attribute becoming most important. Desperation will not assist you; nor must you succumb to depression. Remaining calm will allow you to accept the situation in front of you and assist you in finding peace with the outcome.

We have witnessed this truth playing out in the aftermath of powerful natural disasters—for example, tornadoes, hurricanes, tsunamis, and earthquakes. In these situations, we hear stories of heroism related over and over again. Perhaps, then, the real definition of heroes are those people who have the ability to remain calm, think through a situation, and act in the best interests of all involved in order to bring everyone to safety.

In situations of violent mass shootings or acts of terrorism, we see that remaining calm and thinking clearly have allowed some to be saved that might not have been. We also see that the comfort given by remaining calm, despite knowing the final outcome may be tragic, has given peace to those involved.

Staying calm: Not allowing a stressful situation to overtake sound judgment or cloud one's decisions regarding what needs to be done. This is the attribute that can bring you peace when there is no solution to be had. The abridged definition would be, "It is what it is."

WORKSHEET ON ACHIEVING CALMNESS

How do you see the attribute of CALMNESS in yourself demonstrated to others?

To allow CALMNESS to be visible to others, you must first feel it in yourself.

> How can you help foster CALMNESS in yourself?

Once you know CALMNESS is a part of who you are:

> What challenges does your work environment have that inhibit your CALMNESS?
>
> What challenges does your home environment have that inhibit your CALMNESS?

How can you strengthen your CALMNESS?
> At work
> At home

Goals to bring your CALMNESS to the forefront:
> At work
> At home

If you are unable to exhibit CALMNESS, what do you need to do to move forward to make it possible for others to see calmness in you?
> At work?
> At home?

How will having CALMNESS change your life?
> At work?
> At home?

Chapter Fifteen

Attribute #7: Acknowledge Others

The Fairy Tale Version

A more recent fairy tale introduces us to a princess-to-be who lives in a cartoon world and is an eternal optimist but who is, nonetheless, an independent soul who stands true to her convictions. She is banished to the real world by the evil Queen. Through her adventures in the real world, she acknowledges those around her who help her to realize her dreams. No one is too small, too cynical, or too "real" for this princess-to-be to listen to. She may correct their perceptions, but she always acknowledges that everyone has the right to their feelings, whatever they might be. Her ability to do this allows her to find her true love in the real world and change her life course forever.

The less desirable, alternate version would find our almost-princess discounting those around her who want to help her realize her dreams and discover what her true feelings are. She would never discover her true love and instead would return to her fairy-tale world. She probably would live unhappily ever after with the prince she initially thought she was falling in love with.

In the real word, the ability to acknowledge others who can help us allows us to explore our world in greater depth and take more risks. In doing so, we start to learn what is truly important to us in our lives. As that process happens, the things that are superficial fall by the wayside.

The Modern Era Empowered Woman

In our real world and in a not-so-long-ago past, there lived a beautiful woman by the name of Pocahontas. She was the daughter of a Native American chief and was one of the first to encounter the European explorers that came to find a new life in the New World.

This was a stressful time for the natives of the New World, yet Pocahontas met the challenge with calm and resolve, acknowledging the newcomers with respect and grace. Her acknowledgment of the European visitors allowed her to help others in her community understand these new people. With this attribute of acknowledging others, she helped bridge the cultural differences that divided the two peoples. Her ability to navigate the situation with poise, serenity, and respect allowed a friendship and trust to develop that then allowed these new settlers to continue to explore the new land.

Although this relationship would have negative results for the Native Americans at a later time, the immediate result was that the two groups co-existed peacefully. Had Pocahontas not initiated a peaceful start and acknowledged the strangers' presence, the Native Americans might all have been killed immediately. The chance for these two cultures to eventually understand each other never would have happened.

Acknowledging others means you have the humility to accept that others have good ideas and may know more than you in any particular area. It doesn't mean that either you or they are stupid or that you will be perceived as a leader who is ignorant.

The Antithesis

Women in today's world who are remiss in acknowledging a team member can come across as arrogant. Remember, arrogance is the opposite of humility. Again, we see how all of these attributes work together and at times are intertwined; it's difficult to tease out where one attribute finishes and another begins. Arrogant women who fail to acknowledge others at the workplace or at home often hold the false belief that, by demonstrating this form of authority, they can command respect. Again, nothing is further from the truth. On the contrary, this behavior only continues to generate the feeling that women in leadership positions who behave like this are nothing more than masculinized females acting like bitches.

My Experience

The female head of a program at a hospital where I worked a few years ago was presenting case reports and subsequent results on a particular therapy to a group of healthcare workers. Here was a woman in a leadership position who was feared more than respected. Unfortunately, she did not adhere to some of the values listed in this book. She wouldn't be considered an empowered woman, but quite the opposite.

After she presented the results and conclusions about the effectiveness of this treatment, someone pointed out to her that perhaps her conclusions were faulty because she had omitted an important side effect of the therapy. She immediately dismissed this person and actually responded that perhaps they had administered the therapy incorrectly. Despite the evidence that was presented by this person, which was nationally based, she continued to dismiss what they had to say because it contradicted her faulty judgment.

Her inability to acknowledge another person who had facts she omitted (or perhaps did not know existed) demonstrated her lack of effectiveness as an empowered woman and leader in her field. Had she acknowledged what was being pointed out to her, she would have come across as a person who listens, takes all evidence into account, and incorporates all knowledge to come to appropriate conclusions.

Another downfall of arrogance is the belief that the way in which you have handled a situation in the past is good enough. Sometimes, though, it isn't good enough—in fact, it might be downright wrong. Such arrogance can lead to wrong decisions being made that may affect others in a harmful way. Medical decisions come to mind, of course, but this can apply to any circumstance in any workplace.

My Advice

Although I have been emphasizing that men have a difficult time accepting women who are empowered in their work positions, I also want to emphasize that there are plenty of women who already have positions of power but aren't truly empowered. These are women who may have attained their positions through attributes that are the opposite of those described in this book. These women are in power, but not empowered, which is a very clear distinction. They aren't respectful, nor are they humble. They aren't compassionate, do not work as part of a team, and certainly do not stay calm during moments of stress. Some women lack combinations of these traits, and some have none at all.

It's important to know that a woman must have all of these traits to be considered truly empowered. Otherwise, she will become unbalanced. Depending on which trait is weaker, she will succumb to a more masculine form of leadership rather than the balanced leadership of someone who is truly empowered in all areas of her life.

At home, acknowledging your partner is an important part of a successful relationship. Not doing so will make your partner feel undervalued and unappreciated. You must be able to voice acknowledgement of what you each bring to the table, day-to-day. Never take someone for granted; it breeds contempt.

The opposite is also true. As stated above, you also must be acknowledged for what you have accomplished. It's always a two-way street.

If you read the home economic books presented to girls in high school during the 1950s, you will find unbelievable and outrageous advice for women concerning how to keep a man happy. The writers included advice such as having all the housework done before he got home; ensuring that the children were already fed, clean, and quietly waiting for him; and never presenting any problems to him until he had a chance to eat and relax. There is no room for acknowledgment of the woman from the man, only the other way around. This doesn't make for a happy marriage or a successful partnership in raising a family, let alone promote respect through the acknowledgment of each other's strengths.

It's amazing that any marriage survived back then. Unfortunately, Valium and alcohol were the drugs of choice for many women in those days, helping them tolerate the intolerable.

Are we that much different today? Yes, we have more opportunities in the workplace; however, the job of wife as well as childcare continues to fall squarely on our shoulders, in most relationships. The expectation continues to be that it's our responsibility to make sure the house is well kept and the kids are well taken care of. It's still a rare situation where we find that the man will step up to the plate to share the household and child-rearing responsibilities.

These role descriptions are so ingrained in all our psyches that we, as women, still feel the need to "bring home the bacon, fry it up in a pan." Anything short of this makes us feel like failures. Hence, we see classic examples of depression creep in because we can't do it all and be all to everyone, including ourselves. The fact that we need to prove our worth is so ingrained in us that we don't even think to ask for help. However, if our spouse doesn't offer to help, we become angry because that person did nothing to assist us. How was our mate to know? The other person isn't a mind reader, after all, and probably didn't have the benefit of growing up in an environment that modeled equality of all roles.

And so, the cycle continues until finally we become too exhausted to do anything. We end up asking for mental health days or collapse in a hysterical heap. This, of course, adds more fuel to the fire that women are just hysterical beings who need to be coddled. What could have prevented all this? Prevention would have come in the form of each person acknowledging the other, their strengths and their weakness, their triumphs and their failures—and helping each other with all of the day-to-day life responsibilities.

Acknowledge Others: The ability to listen to other members of the team, perhaps of another group, as well as your partner, and to incorporate their thoughts and ideas as valuable information, all the while accomplishing the goals you have all set out to do.

WORKSHEET ON ACKNOWLEDGING OTHERS

How do you see the attribute of ACKNOWLEDGING OTHERS in yourself demonstrated to others?

To allow ACKNOWLEDGING OTHERS to be visible to others, you must first feel it in yourself.

> How can you help foster ACKNOWLEDGING OTHERS in yourself?

Once you know ACKNOWLEDGING OTHERS is a part of who you are:

> What challenges does your work environment have that inhibit your ACKNOWLEDGEMENT OF OTHERS?

> What challenges does your home environment have that inhibit your ACKNOWLEDGEMENT OF OTHERS?

How can you strengthen your ACKNOWLEGMENT OF OTHERS?
> At work
> At home

Goals to bring your ability to ACKNOWLEDGE OTHERS to the forefront:
> At work
> At home

If you are unable to exhibit the attribute of ACKNOWLEDGING OTHERS, what do you need to do to move forward to make it possible for others to see you begin to acknowledge others?
> At work
> At home

How will having the attribute of ACKNOWLEDGING OTHERS change your life?
   At work
   At home

Chapter Sixteen

Attribute #8: Be Honest

The Fairy Tale Version

Once upon a time, in a fictional exotic land, there lived another princess. Her father, a kindhearted man, ruled her country, which was situated in the Arabian Desert. The story revolves around the princess's reluctance to marry just any suitor simply because he happened to be royalty. One day, she met by chance a young beggar who impersonated a prince. Our desert princess fell in love with him—not because he was a prince but because of his keen sense of adventure. When she discovered he lied to her about being a prince, she wanted nothing to do with him, and so he had to win her trust all over again.

In the not-so-happy ending, the princess might not care that she was lied to and would decide to marry this young man anyway. Of course, their secret would have to remain with them because the rest of the kingdom and certainly her father could not find out he was really just a beggar boy. If anyone discovered his true identity, both he and the princess probably would be executed. So their lies and deception would have to become more and more elaborate until one day, the truth would finally catch up with them. Then they would have to escape and live in exile forever. Her father would die brokenhearted, and the kingdom would fall into evil hands, without any hope for goodness to return.

In the real word, the old adage, "The truth shall set you free," is powerful advice in a world that can so easily accept non-truths for the sake of a better life, fame, or money—take your pick! In the end, a life or career built on lies is like a house of cards that will fall with just a slight breeze.

Lack of honesty can stem from many reasons. For example, arrogance can cloud a leader's judgment so that the truth about a particular situation is hidden. The consequences of such actions can wreak havoc on a company or a country. A famous quote from a movie comes to mind when thinking about this situation: "You want the truth? You can't handle the truth." This is arrogance at its best.

The Modern Era Empowered Woman

Susan B. Anthony is the modern-day woman I would like to draw your attention to as a champion of honesty. She was also a prominent American civil rights leader who played a pivotal role in the Suffrage movement in the United States. She took a prominent role in the New York anti-slavery and temperance movements.

Anthony was outspoken about her distaste of alcohol and morphine-laden patent medicines that were commonly being abused. This is especially important to note because, at that time, much of the advertising that would have supported her journal, *The Revolution*, was sponsored by these so-called medicines. She refused their support, even if it meant the publication would go under.

She was a champion of the rights of all as proclaimed in the Constitution. Her drive to assure equality to all was spurred on by her honesty. Others may have wanted to squash that sentiment because it brought them more power. If you crush your opponent by deeming them inferior, you have achieved superiority over them. However, she understood the truth: that everyone was created equal and, as such, deserved equal rights in everything, including equal pay and the right to vote. She wanted to achieve her goals with the same integrity she believed in and not allow deceitful advertisement to make her goals any less worthy.

The Antithesis

When modern-day women lack honesty, all bets are off. Lies and deception perpetuate erroneous conclusions. Possible life-changing decisions may be made that affect a person's life or a company's future.

Imagine that, because of a lack of honesty, a wrong treatment might be prescribed and a patient may be harmed for life.

At home, a lack of honesty can result in loss of trust and the dissolution of that partnership. Once trust is lost, either at the workplace or at home, it's very difficult to win back and may actually be impossible. Even though this is true of both men and women, I want to highlight that, with women, a lack of honesty can be as damaging—if not more. This is because, in our society, the characteristic of being honest seems to be much more associated with the female persona. Perhaps that is why gossip, which tends to be associated with females, is so damaging to both the person being gossiped about and the person spreading the gossip.

My Experience

A few years ago, another female colleague of mine, also practicing in a different state, told me her story about when she accepted a patient from a male colleague at another hospital within that state. This doctor had kept the patient at his hospital for days, despite recommendations from consultants on the case to transfer the patient as soon as possible. This particular doctor was very arrogant, and his arrogance clouded his assessment of the patient, therefore allowing an erroneous diagnosis and treatment to occur. His arrogance further resulted in his need to be dishonest about the level of care he could provide to the patient.

The patient was finally transferred to my friend's facility in dire straits. She immediately needed to place this patient on life-saving, artificial life support. Unfortunately, despite how aggressive the team was, the patient eventually died. The consensus from all who were involved in the patient's care as well as those that reviewed the case was that, had this patient been transferred sooner, it was possible the team could have saved the patient's life. As you can imagine, my friend was devastated.

This particular physician's dishonesty with the family was not letting them know that the patient should have been transferred to another facility. His dishonesty stemmed from his arrogance in believing he could do everything, when in fact that was not the case.

A life was lost, a family grieved. How do you repair this?

Unfortunately, nothing more could be done for this family. Unfortunately, from what my friend has recently told me, she doesn't believe this particular physician has learned or will ever learn from this tragic case. In fact, a similar situation has repeated itself with the same male physician. Again, another patient was kept too long at his facility. Again, this patient needed to be moved to another facility that was able to provide an increased level of care. Again, the patient was moved too late and, also, eventually died.

As she told me the story, I couldn't help but think this couldn't have happened again; it must be a case of déjà vu. The difference is that in this later case, the head of the department at the hospital the patient was transferred to became aware of the situation. He saw firsthand what this physician was doing and was aghast at the situation as well as the implications of this patient not being offered life-saving technology earlier. The arrogant physician told the family that the patient did not qualify for this therapy, when in fact the patient really did. This story also ended tragically for the patient and family.

Thankfully, others now in a position to remedy this situation are aware of the problem, and perhaps something will be done so that future patients are not imperiled. The sad part, however, is that no one initially believed the woman physician handling the first case described above. It took a male physician to acknowledge that there was a problem—that this particular physician's assessment of the severity of patients' illness, as well as his arrogant belief that he could do everything, resulted in poor care and deadly outcomes for at least two of his patients. How many patients have suffered because of other equally arrogant healthcare workers? How many patients have survived but received lower quality care with less than adequate outcomes, all because arrogance instead of honesty was involved in their healthcare decision-making? In today's world of innovative medicine, with the technologies readily available to us, it's a travesty that these situations even exist. One patient is one too many to receive poor care that impacts their life and or hastens their death.

My Advice

There are those—both men and women—who will never learn from their mistakes because their egos are too big to let them see the truth in situations like these. They refuse to see that there are others who could do more than they could, and they are too arrogant to see beyond their own titles and degrees. These people should be removed from situations that could harm others. In any situation where a woman's opinion rings true yet a man's opinion is heeded by others because he is male, we will continue to run into unpleasant confrontations with possibly dire consequences. My point is that it really doesn't matter if the arrogance originates from a man or a woman; arrogance is wrong, period. However, if the arrogance comes from a man and a woman is the honest person who bravely speaks the truth, we then have the added insult that a potentially harmful situation wasn't averted simply because of the perception that the man is always right. Scenarios like this should never exist if we are truly equalitarian. Unfortunately, they do exist. I hear the stories from other women colleagues and I myself see it firsthand. We most definitely are not equalitarian—far from it.

On the home front, honesty is the best policy. Examples include being honest about how the other person makes you feel as well as being honest about what each other's goals are in life. Without honesty, a relationship will only be smoke and mirrors and, at best, stagnant in its growth.

Honesty trumps arrogance and ego. Only through honesty can a relationship grow, prosper, and achieve goals that serve both the individual and the couple. Let me tell you bluntly that a relationship without honesty is doomed to complete failure and should be ended.

A case in point would be a partner who is cheating. This would demonstrate dishonesty in the most intimate characteristics of a relationship. In another example, dishonesty in the financial aspects of a relationship is, in fact, the most common reason that couples break up. (Forbes.com 1/13/2011, Jenna Goudreau, "Is your Partner Cheating on You Financially?")

Finally, dishonesty regarding your true feelings for the other person will eventually lead to the demise of that relationship.

Of course, it's obvious that two people being honest with each other can prevent all these examples I just described. Yet, we continue to see these situations play out time and time again in relationships, despite each partner knowing the hazards of being dishonest. So how is it possible that, when we know the consequences of being dishonest, we continue to see dishonesty practiced? Can denial about the truth be so powerful that the person who is being dishonest truly believes he is in the right? Does that person really believe his or her lies are the truth?

Perhaps the following can help us answer some of these questions. Let's go back to the essence of this book for a moment and examine how this can be better understood.

Almost since the beginning of time, men have been given the sovereign right to rule. Power is very tempting and can influence actions that otherwise would not be taken if a collaborative effort existed and if all people were respected for their thoughts and ideas. After all, to be dishonest also constitutes being disrespectful to other human beings, as noted above. However, here's the clincher: if the other human being is a woman, the perception by men in power seems to be that no disrespect or dishonesty has been committed. They were simply acting in accordance with the rule that men are always right and are not to be questioned.

I believe these are the powerful forces that can enter into day-to-day life in personal relationships and at work. That is why we see all the situations described in this chapter continuing to exist. This type of dishonesty, and all of its ramifications, will only begin to fade away when an equalitarian society becomes the rule rather than the exception.

I also want to emphasize again how much these attributes are tied together. To be honest also means you respect the other person. Respect begets acknowledgment of their efforts. Acknowledgment doesn't allow arrogance to creep in, and therefore we return to the opposite of arrogance--humility—which is a prerequisite for respect of others' opinions.

Honesty: The trait that brings truth to the table and allows appropriate decisions to be made in all aspects of life. Being honest naturally allows respect to also be part of the relationship, both at home and at work.

WORKSHEET ON HONESTY

How do you see the attribute of HONESTY in yourself demonstrated to others?

To allow HONESTY to be visible to others, you must first feel it in yourself.

> How can you help foster HONESTY in yourself?

Once you know HONESTY is a part of who you are:

> What challenges does your work environment have that inhibit your HONESTY?
>
> What challenges does your home environment have that inhibit your HONESTY?

How can you strengthen your HONESTY?
> At work
> At home

Goals to bring your HONESTY to the forefront:
> At work
> At home

If you are unable to exhibit HONESTY, what do you need to do to move forward to make it possible for others to see honesty in you?
> At work
> At home

How will having HONESTY change your life?
> At work
> At home

Chapter Seventeen

Attribute #9: Demonstrate Courage

The Fairy Tale Version

Once upon a time, near a forest long ago, lived two little children—a brother and sister. Because of a famine, the father and abusive stepmother took the children into the forest and abandoned them there. Lost and alone, the children wandered around until they came to a pretty cottage made of sweets. They discovered—too late—that a hungry witch inhabited it. The children were locked up in cages and fed by the witch to fatten them up.

It would appear there was no escape; however, the little girl grabbed the opportunity to courageously trick the witch. When the witch took the girl out of the cage and told her to crawl into the oven, the girl acted as if she didn't understand what she was supposed to do. The witch demonstrated how to get inside the oven, and the girl pushed the witch into the oven, killing her. She then released her brother. They found precious jewels in the house, which they took. Eventually, they made their way back home, where they discovered their evil stepmother had died. The father was overjoyed to see them and, with their newfound wealth, they lived happily ever after.

In a less-happy ending, the sister would have been too scared to attempt to trick the witch. The brother and sister would have died at the witch's hand. The father eventually would have died too, a lonely, heartbroken man—and that would have been the end of this tragic story. It was the sister's courage, against all odds, that saved this family.

In the real world, we see many acts of courage by women in everyday life. For example, fighting cancer while still serving as a mom, a wife, or a businesswoman or employee demonstrates the courage to battle an illness with grace.

Fighting against the indignities placed upon women in certain parts of this world, as I have described before, shows courage in the face of the possibility of being killed for one's beliefs.

The Modern Era Empowered Woman

I have chosen to highlight three courageous women because each deserves accolades for what she selflessly has done for others. Perhaps that is the true definition of courage: fighting adversity for the good of others, regardless of how that may impact you as an individual. This has been the hardest attribute to write about, because courage can be elusive and found in small acts that might go unnoticed by many.

Here are three of the many women I believe embody courage:

Erin Brokovitch demonstrated courage by persistently calling out a corporation for the destruction it caused to the environment and the harm it did to the surrounding community. Although the corporation attempted to silence her many times, she continued her fight and eventually brought justice to the affected community. She continues to be the voice of justice and courage, fighting large corporations that harm the environment or the people within the communities they serve. She has won many battles, and is well respected for the work she did and continues to do across the U.S.

Amelia Earhart is another woman who exemplifies the attribute of courage. Her courage was shown in her drive to conquer flight as a woman—an achievement that was impressive in and of itself. She further showed her courage in flying solo across the ocean. Although her life ended tragically, she nonetheless demonstrated that courage as part of empowerment can help you reach your goals. Her present-day relative and namesake has completed Amelia's flight plan and also joined the ranks of truly empowered women.

Malala Yousafzai is the young Pakistani girl I mentioned earlier, who spoke up for the right of girls and women to receive an education. For her outspoken and courageous nature, she was shot in the face and left for dead. The attempt to silence her backfired: because of what happened to her, women in Pakistan seem to have gained a small victory. The drive to bring education to girls, although still risky, continues to thrive. Perhaps it will become the norm rather than the exception.

The Antithesis

Women who lack courage typically do not speak out about crimes being done to themselves, their co-workers, or their children. These are women who have been physically, mentally, or verbally abused and do not have the courage to denounce the cowards behaving negatively towards them. Lack of courage can result in continued abuse and can perpetuate the stigma placed on women as the weaker sex. It can destroy self-confidence and all hope to make the world a better place. Lack of courage elevates the abuser to a position of power and doesn't allow righteous behavior to appear.

My Experience

I must admit that, as hard as this attribute is to write about, it's equally difficult to personally describe. As an example, I believe you can witness courage in young girls who are bullied at school but continue to maintain their dignity and move past the abuse to achieve greatness.

Perhaps courage is so elusive that we only see it in snippets of the daily life of physicians, when they must tell families and patients that the end is near. When physicians withdraw life support, you can be a witness to courageous acts of compassion. Assisting the end of suffering and providing comfort to families through this sadness isn't playing God; it's the express responsibility of our oath: "First, do no harm." Delaying the inevitable continues to harm the patient through prolonging pain. It also harms the family by giving false hope for recovery when there is none to be had.

In business, women can demonstrate courage by alerting coworkers about improper business practices that might impact them or others adversely. They also can show their courage by protecting other women from the ravages of male domination in the workplace. Not allowing sexual harassment to happen takes courage. It is neither easy nor particularly pleasant to stand up to the male bullies at work who continue to propagate such practices as normal and expected.

Perhaps the deepest form of courage can be seen in our servicewomen—not only those in the military, protecting our freedom, but also our police and firefighters who continuously risk their lives to serve the public. We usually equate these acts of courage with men; however, the unsung female heroes in these roles should never be pushed aside or forgotten. They are powerful examples of physical and emotional courage on display to serve others.

At home, examples of courage can be seen when women leave domestic abuse situations despite the risk of being found and beaten.

My Advice

Cultivating courage is difficult at best. I believe a natural spark needs to exist within us to fuel the ability to grow courage. Do we all have it? I believe we do. How else could we, as women, attempt to leave the supposed comforts of being taken care of by men to live a life of adventure—a life full of surprises and a life fraught with hardships—for the sake of working in a man's world?

Perhaps the best way to bring courage to the surface is to place yourself in the position of the person you are attempting to help. Would you want another human being to ignore your plea for help? If the answer is no, how could you turn a blind eye and not help? Remember that "doing unto others as you would want them to do unto you" still applies to our modern era. Some situations might be difficult; they might involve risking your job or even your life. No doubt, having courage in any situation is never easy, but well worth those difficulties. The result is that it allows your empowerment to grow even stronger. It will set you apart from others who can't make those hard decisions.

Every empowered woman has this attribute. Perhaps it remains hidden most times. However, when the need arises, you will see it surface and be a force to be reckoned with. The fear that may temporarily wash over you can easily be pushed aside when you realize the needs of others far surpass the possible risks you might incur if you perform the necessary courageous act.

I believe the only way to strengthen the attribute of courage is to face problems head on—not hide or run away from them. You may find that you aren't alone in your quest to demonstrate courageous behavior. You will be encouraged not only by the appreciation of those you are helping but also by the knowledge that you are truly making a difference in your community, and, eventually, the world in general.

Courage is contagious. When one person demonstrates this attribute, you will start seeing it blossom in others. Courage perpetuates the belief that the right thing is being done for the sake of others.

Courage: The attribute that allows you to act selflessly in situations that are dangerous for you, for the sake of bettering others' situations and improving the world, one person at a time.

WORKSHEET ON DEMONSTRATING COURAGE

How do you see the attribute of COURAGE in yourself demonstrated to others?

To allow COURAGE to be visible to others, you must first feel it in yourself.

How can you help foster COURAGE in yourself?

Once you know COURAGE is a part of who you are:

What challenges does your work environment have that inhibit your ABILITY TO DEMONSTRATE COURAGE?

What challenges does your home environment have that inhibit your ABILITY TO DEMONSTRATE COURAGE?

How can you strengthen your ABILITY TO DEMONSTRATE COURAGE?
    At work
    At home

Goals to bring your COURAGE to the forefront:
    At work
    At home

If you are unable to exhibit COURAGE, what do you need to do to move forward to make it possible for others to see courage in you?
    At work
    At home

How will having COURAGE change your life?
    At work
    At home

Chapter Eighteen

Attribute #10: Achieve Success

The Fairy Tale Version

Once upon a time, in a world under the sea, there lived a rebellious and curious young mermaid. She wanted more out of a life than being a mermaid. She wanted adventure and to succeed in the world above the sea. Her goal was to figure out a way to successfully learn to live on land. She wanted this so much that all of her efforts were geared to that end result. Although she endured many hardships and setbacks, eventually she achieved her goal of a happy life on land.

In the alternate, not-so-happy version, this young mermaid would feel ambivalent about continuing to improve who she is or achieving the goals she sets for herself. She would therefore languish in the sea and never discover another world, and she would never challenge herself to create a successful life.

In the real world, we all know of people who don't believe in themselves and therefore never strive to make something better of their lives. They stay in the status quo, complacent and uninspired to succeed in life. That lack of a desire to achieve will keep them from becoming better people or, perhaps, making an important difference in others' lives or in their community.

The value in wanting to succeed isn't in achieving fame and fortune, although these benefits certainly could be part of the outcome. The importance is to yourself, in knowing that your hard work and desire to achieve success is the true payback. Where would the world be if no one had the motivation to be successful in his or her endeavors? I daresay, we would not have the advancement of knowledge or technology we have today.

The Modern Era Empowered Woman

Two women immediately come to mind that demonstrate the achievement of unsurpassed success. I'm talking about Sally Ride and Christa McAuliffe. Both of these courageous women entered a field essentially dominated by men. Space exploration has always been a man's domain, yet through their perseverance and hard work, Ride and McAuliffe achieved success in being part of the elite U.S astronaut program. They ventured to a place few of us have had the pleasure to see firsthand. They opened the world's eyes to the level of achievement women can attain. They became instant, phenomenal role models to young girls everywhere—girls who may have been told they could never be good at math or science just because they were girls, but who now had the hope to achieve their dreams. They became instantly "cool" role models to those girls who have been ridiculed for being smart and, therefore, considered geeks.

The Antithesis

Lacking the desire to achieve success will keep the modern-day woman behind in all areas of her life. This lack of ambition to be successful in her endeavors will relegate her to being mediocre at whatever she does. Her lackluster attitude will then further corrode any semblance of wanting to better her life, whether at work or at home. Saying "It's good enough" doesn't allow for attempting to achieve success, for success is never just good enough—it's the best you can be in any given situation.

My Experience

Let me use an example I have more experience with. There are nurses and allied healthcare workers who come to work day after day, take orders from residents and doctors, and do an adequate job taking care of a patient. Alternately, I have the privilege to work with many nurses and allied healthcare workers that come to work empowered in their ability to discuss patient care issues with the medical team, of which they are always a part. They provide their patients not with "adequate" care but with care that shows compassion and respect. They enjoy their work so much more; they are a team player and exude confidence in their nursing or healthcare skills. They are always compassionate toward their patients and patients' families and remain calm during moments of crisis when they are assisting the medical team. They acknowledge that others might have a different set of knowledge skills but, again, they are confident in their assessment of their patients' progress toward recovery.

There is a marked difference that comes about when success is part of the whole picture that empowers you as a woman to lead others—or, at the very least, to be considered a valuable part of the team. The goal of achieving success in the business world is equally important to discuss. Here we can see potential difficulties when the achievement of a particular successful outcome isn't because of the above attributes, as I have talked about, but instead because of negative traits that guide such success.

One example would be the use of unethical means to gain a successful result. Another example would be the use of power instead of empowerment to demand that others work a certain way or do something not agreeable to everyone on the team.

Success often is equated with power, and, again, this influence can wreak havoc on what is truly important in the process of acquiring whatever success you are seeking. Please be mindful that power corrupts both men and women alike. The perception of having power can cloud your decision-making abilities, your ethics, and your humanity. You will know when you are in its throes because the people around you will fear you, not value or respect you. It's very important to make this distinction early on as well as throughout the process of acquiring success, lest you fall into the allure of power and lose your value system entirely.

My Advice

Do you think it's curious that I would label success as an attribute rather than the ultimate goal of an empowered woman? If you actually think about, success is what drives us to become effectual, empowered leaders. The goals we set are the framework for how we achieve them. We achieve them through the attributes previously described that lead to wanting to have success in our endeavors.

This might sound like a circular argument, but think about it: we want to be empowered women leaders as a result of all these attributes, including achieving success. I daresay I do not want us to become powerful women. Those previous examples I have described in the world of business are as frightening as the stories of men who feel their power isn't to be questioned.

To achieve success as an empowered woman means you are striving to make the world a better place, whether through industry, through individual people (as in medicine), or at home by helping to create a successful partnership.

If you lack this attribute, you'll have the same experience as our young mermaid—daily activities become mundane. All else was unimportant to her except for striving to succeed in living on land. The same is true for us. If we set no goals, there is no need for the above attributes to guide us to become empowered leaders. As women, we can easily fall into this trap by the stereotypical roles in which we are placed—such as secretary, waitress, homemaker, nurse, or store clerk. Yet, each of these positions can be empowered by cultivating the eleven attributes. When the goal of wanting success in whatever you do is present, those stereotypical roles can become important, not just mundane roles performed by rote.

At home, success translates to a well-functioning home life, partner, and kids that live within a functional, not dysfunctional, family. Success as a homemaker (which, by the way, is a real job) shows in the ability to keep the family unit together, united in the goal of creating a fulfilled life full of wonderful memories. Successful families produce children who grow up and aspire to become respected and needed members of society who contribute to a better life for themselves and others.

Let me be clear, however, on one point—I consider both partners living under one roof as "homemakers," and not just the woman of the house. In other words, both partners equally contribute to the success of that family unit. I refer the reader to my examples in the chapter on acknowledgment. As a woman homemaker, we need to even more clearly define the job—not just as housekeeping, grocery shopping, feeding the kids, and keeping our partner happy, but also as truly making a difference in the successful growth of that family. That is why I strive to be clear in these descriptions, especially since women have been relegated to being homemakers for so many years and, historically, the job description has been equated to menial work, equal to a housekeeper's position. As women, we know it's so much more!

By using all the attributes, you can see how being a homemaker can be both inspiring and empowering. Demonstrating this empowerment to your partner will also cement in that person's perception the importance of what you do at home, thereby eliminating the attitude that what you do is menial work.

If this attribute of achieving success is lacking, using the other attributes for empowerment becomes a moot point. Why bother? As noted above, we see this in the example of how a nurse can either go through her daily activities in a rut or change her attitude and use the attributes to become a woman empowered in her career. We also see it on the home front, where "woman's work" is actually elevated to an empowered lifestyle choice because of its importance in today's world.

Success: The attribute that helps drive your goal of using all the other attributes to become an empowered woman. It's the attribute that guides you daily to make a better person of yourself personally and at work. Again, I want to emphasize an important, critical distinction: success doesn't equate to power. Power can lead to success, but by the wrong means. We do not live in a Machiavellian society. The ends do not and should not justify the means—ever.

WORKSHEET ON ACHIEVING SUCCESS

How do you see the attribute of SUCCESS in yourself demonstrated to others?

To allow SUCCESS to be visible to others, you must first feel it in yourself.

>How can you help foster SUCCESS in yourself?

Once you know SUCCESS is a part of who you are:

>What challenges does your work environment have that inhibit your ABILITY TO ACHIEVE SUCCESS?

>What challenges does your home environment have that inhibit your ABILITY TO ACHIEVE SUCCESS?

How can you strengthen your ABILITY TO ACHIEVE SUCCESS?
>At work
>At home

Goals to bring the attribute of ACHIEVING SUCCESS to the forefront:
>At work
>At home

If you are unable to exhibit the attribute of ACHIEVING SUCCESS, what do you need to do to move forward to make it possible for others to see you achieve success?
>At work
>At home

How will ACHIEVING SUCCESS change your life?
>At work
>At home

Chapter Nineteen

Attribute #11: Enjoy Your Work

The Fairy Tale Version

Once upon a time, there lived a very tiny little girl. Even though normal-sized humans raised her, she enjoyed her life as a little person and all the complexities of the world around her that only she could appreciate from her tiny-sized perception. She never wanted to become normal-sized; she loved what she was and relished every adventure it brought her. After a series of encounters with other tiny creatures, she met and married someone her own size: a tiny fairy prince.

The flip side of this story would find this miniature girl trying desperately to find a means to make herself normal-sized, all the while missing out on the beauty of her tiny world.

In the real world, we have all met people who work only so they can enjoy retirement and never enjoy each moment along the way. We might even know people who, by the time they reach retirement, die suddenly and never enjoy retirement (or life) at all—what a sad way to live. Living in the moment is a difficult concept to understand and practice, but a crucial one nonetheless. Although it's important to keep your sights on your goals and strive to achieve them, it's equally important to enjoy the journey.

The Modern Era Empowered Woman

What better example of a person who was able to enjoy life to the fullest than someone who lacked two of her senses: sight and hearing.

Helen Keller demonstrated to the world that life was to be enjoyed to the fullest with the capacity we have been given to enjoy it. Here is a woman who was blind and deaf from childhood. She learned from a wonderful teacher, early on, that she had the choice of going through life feeling tremendously sorry for herself and being miserable because of what she lacked, or she could learn to experience life and the world around her with her other senses, on another level that normal people lacked. Her appreciation of her world was enhanced by her other senses. She lived a life full of wonder and helped others recognize the beauty all around them.

The Antithesis

Today's woman who lacks the ability to enjoy her life will either do things by rote or be disgruntled and sour in all her personal dealings. She will swim in an ocean of self-pity and never understand the simple joys in life. If she is driven to reach a certain goal, she will be unable to enjoy the journey that takes her to her end result, thereby stealing chunks of her life away. By the time she reaches her destination, even though success has been attained, this success will feel less desirable because the journey was so onerous.

My Experience

I recently asked a friend of mine how she enjoyed her profession. Her immediate response was that she hated every second she was at work. I was flabbergasted.

For the most part, I believe you will hear this type of statement less often from female professionals. As females, we have to juggle and compromise between our work and our families. If we hated what we did, it would be nearly impossible to do our work safely or effectively. But, unfortunately, it does happen at times to both men and women alike.

Imagine going to work every day of your life and hating what you do. Imagine the physical ills that stem from mentally being so very unhappy. I have also seen physicians where I work go through the motions of taking care of their patients but never truly realizing the impact their care has on others. Their perception is that they are doing their job, not making a difference in others' lives. The unfortunate part here is that not only are they not enjoying what they do, their care can be less than adequate because they do not see the value in the work they do.

Learning to appreciate and love what you do is as important as all the other attributes we have previously discussed.

Let me further illustrate the point. There is a restaurant that was created by and is run by blind people. The restaurant itself is completely dark. Customers are led to their tables by their servers, order from a verbal menu, and eat their food completely in the dark, unable to see what they are eating. The reviews have been phenomenal. People who eat there often leave with a whole different perspective on life in general. Their comments range from the simple experience of how enhanced the food tastes to a more general feeling that they have, indeed, been missing out on different aspects of their lives by not stopping to truly enjoy each moment. These are the types of experiences that jolt us awake so that the beauty of the journey isn't lost in striving to achieve the destination.

These are difficult lessons to learn and, as I have mentioned above, they aren't always learned in time.

My Advice

We all could learn a tremendously important lesson from this attribute. Love the person you are, gather strength from all your talents and accomplishments, and enjoy your life! You have only one; you can't re-create it or go back and relive it. It is what it is.

We must be able to enjoy what we do. We must see value in our work and see that what we do makes the world a better place. I don't care if you're flipping burgers, emptying trash, or cleaning toilets—each person's job is valuable to many others. Without everyone doing their share at home and in the workplace, the final product (whether it's producing an item, raising children, or providing excellent healthcare) can't come about. All team members need to be involved, engaged, and happy in their work.

Life doesn't begin when we leave the workplace and end when we enter it the next day. To quote the very sage Ralph Waldo Emerson, "Life is the journey, not the destination." I'm sure you understand that this concept completely translates to home, too. You must enjoy your home life. If not, it's time to re-think it, reconsider what you are or aren't doing, and decide whether it's worth saving or not. It's as clear as that.

Remember, life is short. We are here to make a better world. We are here to better ourselves. We are here to enjoy every moment doing both and to live fulfilled, purposeful lives.

The gift given to us at birth is the ability to be part of a greater creation. We are given the gift of wonder, which we can often see in the simple act of a baby discovering its hand or the world outside its crib. We have an obligation to ourselves and the world around us to create a sacred space, worthy of life itself. The simple joys of what our senses bring us are the road to enjoying the journey of our lives. Please don't waste it on "What if?" or "Why me?"

Enjoyment: Don't waste your precious time on seeking pity and playing the victim. Move on in your life, and remember to see the beauty around you. If you see that what surrounds you needs improvement, help that process become a reality. Anything short of this can only bring you misery, self-pity, and eventual non-fulfillment of your dreams. Yes, you may reach your goal, but the road will be unpleasant, and the end won't bring you the same joy you would find if the journey were the true adventure, and you enjoyed it to your full capacity.

WORKSHEET ON ENJOYING LIFE

How do you see the attribute of ENJOYING LIFE in yourself?

To allow ENJOYMENT OF LIFE to be visible to others, you must first feel it in yourself.

> How can you help foster ENJOYING LIFE in yourself?

Once you know ENJOYMENT OF LIFE is a part of who you are:

> What challenges does your work environment have that inhibit your ability to ENJOY LIFE?
>
> What challenges does your home environment have that inhibit your ability to ENJOY LIFE?

How can you strengthen your ENJOYMENT OF LIFE?
- At work
- At home

Goals to bring your ability to ENJOY LIFE to the forefront:
- At work
- At home

If you are unable to exhibit ENJOYMENT OF LIFE, what do you need to do to move forward to make it possible for others to see this attribute in you?
- At work
- At home

How will having the ability to ENJOY LIFE change your life?
- At work
- At home

Part IV

Chapter Twenty

The Modern Fairy Tale

Once upon a future time, a world exists that was only possible in the dreams of those wanting a better life for all. In this world, there lives a society that affords every possible opportunity to each and every one of its citizens. First and foremost, since infancy, each person's education fills them with the knowledge that all humans have full equality, one with another. Therefore, race, gender, sexual preference, and socioeconomic station have no bearing on their value as humans. All opinions are respected, discussed, and implemented based on the value of the ideas, not who presents them.

It is within reason to believe that this future society runs with increased efficiency and witnesses more peace than has ever been seen at any other time in history. How is this possible? It's possible because of the following.

If we look at the individual family units that make up this future world, we see respectful partners raising their children with a great deal of love and patience. The traditional mother/father role is shared equally, as are the daily routines. Every person's career is viewed as equally important. There are no role distinctions, and greater importance isn't placed on one person over the other. Children grow up with a great deal of respect for every person, so there is no discrimination based on race, religion, income, or sex. Schools teach tolerance and respect for all human beings, and educational opportunities are no longer discriminatory.

Since having power over others is no longer the final goal, education of all citizens becomes important. Cultural differences are celebrated, and everyone learns from others. The uniqueness of each culture is never viewed with suspicion or distaste;

instead, it's a learning experience for all. We do see, however, that even within different cultures, one thread of similarity exists, and that, again, is the inherent respect for every individual, despite differences in factors such as race, sex, or socioeconomic status.

Since education continues to emphasize these qualities, they become second nature to children. Therefore, education creates an equal playing field for all. Education means that no one person or people can "rule" over you because you have been kept in the dark through lack of knowledge. Education leads to innovative ideas, which then lead to new discoveries in all areas, especially medicine and technology. These discoveries in turn create a better world for all, because they don't allow one person or people to be in control of others.

In this new world, men and women are seen as equals. Education has also shown that certain old cultural ideas and customs must be laid to rest, because instead of elevating the human condition, they were created to subjugate women. So female mutilation is now seen as barbaric, having only existed in the past to degrade women in general and to ensure that men had power over women. The thought that women were a commodity to buy or sell—that their only function in life was to procreate and spend a lifetime in servitude to men—becomes extinct. Domestic violence against women also becomes a thing of the past, having occurred only because it was another way to keep women submissive, scared, and powerless over their own lives. Women now can model to their daughters and sons the value within each man and woman. This way of thinking continues to be propagated throughout the generations.

When we see this new way of thinking, we realize that many of the old problems our world faced, such as prostitution of children and women, slave trafficking, and the illicit drug trade, all disappear quickly. Why, might you ask? Why would certain populations see the need to deal in human trafficking and drug dealing in the old world but not the new one?

Again, let's go back to the new way of thinking, the new way of raising children and educating them, and the priorities that are now the norm for this new world. When we look at the world with these new perspectives, life isn't taken for granted, and everyone deserves the best their life can become.

In this new world, as children grow into adults, they bring these values of equality and respect to the workplace. Their companies then continue to embody and channel these values to all their employees. Communication continues to improve exponentially, so that the world truly becomes a village where everyone is interconnected and cares about each other's lives. In essence, communication can only improve because, through education, knowledge increases, which ultimately allows all to have the same life opportunities.

As we ascend the ladder of society, we see that governments and corporations have equal numbers of male and female leaders, and the boards of these corporations also show equal representation. Power is no longer the goal to achieve, nor is the best profit margin the ultimate measure of success. Instead, the outstanding productivity of its citizens and employees, respectively, becomes an organization's most important marker of success, along with the development of innovative products.

When we look at this new world's healthcare system, we see that medicine has achieved astonishing advances, partly from the ability of all professionals to see beyond their own egos, prejudices, and the way things have always been done. Instead, we see innovative theories blossom, being tested, and then put into clinical practice. Because egos have gone by the wayside, patients are appropriately taken care of at dedicated facilities. Because power no longer is the operative word for success, we see hospitals not wanting to retain their patients solely for the bottom line. Therefore, the health of all citizens is at its best, and mortality—especially maternal and infant mortality—is at an all-time low.

Furthermore, advances in pharmaceuticals also play a role in the advancement in medical treatments. Since profit is no longer the ultimate goal, pharmaceuticals are now created to improve everyone's health, and the cost of creating these pharmaceuticals no longer becomes an issue. Previously, the high cost of creating new medicines was attributed to the need for these companies to protect themselves from medical malpractice. Now that this new society understands that complications can occur as a natural part of the disease process, careers are no longer built to protect the creation of the highest profits. Medical malpractice has therefore fallen to the wayside as a method to make a living at another's expense.

Society also understands that therapies are prescribed based on the best knowledge at the time. The cost of medicine decreases as we begin to better understand that quality of life, not life itself, is of the utmost importance. In other words, a person whose time has come to pass is allowed to die with dignity. Life support is given when there is hope for recovery. It isn't given because life must be supported at all costs, incurring continued suffering with no hope of any meaningful recovery. Again, these principles can only become accepted with the education of all citizens about what is considered a meaningful life.

When we evaluate the food supply in this future fairyland, it's plentiful and equally distributed, which in turn has essentially eliminated world hunger. This abundance has occurred because governments no longer need to dominate their citizens. Nations also no longer play the power game where food supplies are rationed depending on how another country acts, or as a form of punishment.

Because starvation no longer occurs, the human brain has the full potential to develop and take advantage of excellent education. This potential leads to continued improvement in the productivity of the world's citizens, and this improved productivity leads not only to increased production of items but also to an increase in ideas and innovation for world change to improve the environment.

Again, profit no longer continues to be what is important; that is, the bottom line isn't considered the most important measure of success. So, since profit no longer rules every decision, all living creatures have a better life, including farm animals. Our natural environment—for example, the rainforest—continues to thrive and replenish the world's oxygen supply and eliminate excess carbon molecules, which previously contributed to global warming. In response, the oceans become healthier, pollution decreases significantly, and excess farming of the oceans and land no longer occurs since these were also done mostly to increase insane profit margins.

So, we see again that respect for our world, its environment, and the people living on this planet becomes one of the most important factors that ensure the success of a continued, plentiful life.

We also see that because profit margins are no longer the most important factor, wars cease to exist. Why would leaders consider sacrificing young lives to the ravages of wars that are fought because of a lack of respect for each other's cultures, or to gain power over one another, or to overtake a country that is deemed dangerous to others? Those situations cease to exist—again, because the dangers were directly tied to using weapons of mass destruction. These concepts no longer exist; therefore, wars no longer exist.

Power becomes an undesirable trait. Power implies that we aren't all equal, that some are more privileged, smarter, and richer and therefore should be the leaders and make decisions for others. This trait goes against all of the previous qualities and desires society has learned to appreciate.

In this new world, religion becomes the means by which we celebrate the spirituality that exists in all of us and celebrate life itself.

I would certainly not call this new world a "brave new world." On the contrary, we are brave to be living the way we do today, faced with the harsh realities that inequality, disrespect, and power seekers bring to the rest of us. This new world would be better named "the elevated world." It's how I believe the world was meant to be.

This elevated world is, unfortunately, truly a fairy tale at this time. And yet, there is a happily ever after. It would consist of no crime against each other, no power struggles, no wars, no hunger, and no lack of education, lack of equality, or lack of respect for each other. The happy ending would be a peaceful, cleaner world where we all have equal rights to our opinions, to an education, to excellent healthcare, and to creating a better life for our families—and, in the process, a better world.

That's the final happy ending. Are we capable of creating it for our future generations? I think we might have a chance if we start slowly, one person at a time.

Each attribute I have described is geared toward bringing awareness of the need for respect for each other; each attribute is geared to elevate equality of the sexes, races, and cultures as the norm rather than the exception. These attributes can bring us closer to this new reality.

Of course, this will not happen overnight. Think about the movie *Pay It Forward*. The concept is simple yet very powerful. It's based on making this world a better place by propagating one small act of kindness. After all, as you have seen in the attributes I've described, kindness is intimately tied to respect and empathy. It's certainly hard to have one without the other.

As each and every one of us pay it forward, we create a small but sure ripple effect throughout society that allows others to see another side—a side filled with respect and gentleness toward one another. This is a world where we can enjoy each other's differences and celebrate each day for the joy it can bring us through the attainment of knowledge and the certainty of knowing we now live in world free of suffering, strife and pain—individually and in society as a whole.

In this new world, the old ways are finally forgotten as relics of a past that did not serve humanity well.

In this new world, we look to the heavens not as a means for salvation but as a testament that life as we used to know it has finally been elevated to a higher purpose. Life is finally closer to what the creator of all living beings and of the universe itself has wanted us to attain all along.

Chapter Twenty-One

Final Thoughts

As I started to write this book, I found that my goals for the message I wanted to deliver changed. Initially, I wanted simply to teach others about the attributes I believed were critical in the development of empowerment for women. I also discovered the importance of including the history of women's inequality and our struggles, past and current. However, as I continued to describe the attributes that would bring about women's empowerment, I realized that, really, the final goal was to create a world where equal rights existed for everyone and where respect was the basis for all interactions.

In fact, writing this book has been cathartic. I finally have been able to verbalize how I have felt all these years, in terms of what I have experienced in dealing with the male members of my profession as well as what I have seen other women physicians go through. In speaking to other professional women, I've learned that many have had similar experiences throughout their careers.

That isn't to say that every male physician I have worked with is, in essence, a power-hungry, disrespectful ass. Many are actually quite modern in that their respect for others doesn't include preconceived sexual inequities. They are respectful of differing opinions and wanting to work within a team to better medical outcomes in patients.

Part of the impetus for writing this book came from my marriage to a wonderful man who has never had any preconceived notions about what women can or can't do. Despite all the craziness I deal with at work, I come home to a loving, respectful relationship where being honored and listened to is present in every action and conversation. I believe that our daughter has had fabulous role models in terms of what equality of the sexes is all about. She can see that, as women, we have the ability to be empowered both at work and at home.

In describing the attributes of empowered women, I also have discovered that there are some women who have used attributes that I would not condone to achieve a level of success in different walks of life despite the prejudices thrown at them. Unfortunately, I believe these successful women were raised in hostile environments where they needed to act viciously in an adversarial, competitive world. They do not know a better way.

This book does show a different way—and, certainly, what I believe to be a better way—to achieve respect in the workplace and in the home. I can only hope that as our daughters enter their professions of choice, they will have a vastly different, more positive experience than my own and that of my female colleagues.

It is my firm belief that the respect we, as women, deserve eventually will become second nature to all of our male colleagues and partners. I believe that eventually they no longer will need any reminders to respect us as the valuable human beings we are. We are a force to be listened to and a force to be reckoned with, both at work and at home. We deserve to be respected as human beings with equal value, whether male or female. It's in this small way that I feel we can begin to better our world and slowly reach the end point of our final fairy tale.

To recap, UNITE together, Sisters, and remember to:

1. Exude confidence.
2. Work as part of the team.

3. Respect others and never compromise.
4. Be compassionate and show empathy.
5. Be humble and always know you are constantly learning.
6. Stay calm during times of stress.
7. Acknowledge others.
8. Display honesty.
9. Demonstrate courage.
10. Have success as your ultimate goal.
11. Enjoy your work.

If we can remember these attributes and nurture them, perhaps we will have a chance to take up the ERA again and see it permanently become a part of the Constitution. Perhaps we will see true respect in the workplace and at home, and perhaps our daughters will have a better chance for a life free from prejudice, derogatory statements, subservient service, or less pay for equal work. Perhaps education for women in other parts of the world will be a given, rather than something to be fought for.

Perhaps, slowly, our world will become a better place to live because of all these changes—one person at a time, one community at a time, through the development of respect and equality for all. It is my fervent hope that this new normal eventually will erase any memory of the old ways and that the world will move toward a future full of promise, innovation, and a successful survival within our universe.

About the Author

Cristina Carballo-Perelman, M.D., has been a neonatologist for over twenty-five years. She and her female colleagues have experienced firsthand many of the misperceptions concerning the capability of women in the workplace. She has seen how society as a whole continues to devalue women both in their careers and at home by placing greater value in beauty over brains. She has also experienced the opposite at home, where her marriage to another physician, is rooted in respect and equality.

Her passion to write this book, therefore, derives from wanting to help this generation of women, including her daughter, who are in the throes of popular culture, to find a better way.

By becoming empowered women, not "little men", she hopes to help accelerate the overall equality of the sexes in all areas of life.

The author lives in Scottsdale, Arizona, with her husband, now a retired physician.

www.ingramcontent.com/pod-product-compliance
Lightning Source LLC
Chambersburg PA
CBHW070423010526
44118CB00014B/1873